THE

VIRGINIA CONVENTION

OF

1829-30

THE

VIRGINIA CONVENTION

OF

1829-30

BY

Hugh Blair Grigsby

DA CAPO PRESS · NEW YORK · 1969

E.T.S.U. AT TEXARKANA LIBRARY

100585

A Da Capo Press Reprint Edition

This Da Capo Press edition of
The Virginia Convention of 1829–30
is an unabridged republication of
the first edition published in
Richmond, Virginia, in 1854.
It is reprinted from a copy of that
edition in the Cornell University
Libraries.

Library of Congress Catalog Card Number 79-75321

Published by Da Capo Press
A Division of Plenum Publishing Corporation
227 West 17th Street
New York, N. Y. 10011
All rights reserved

Manufactured in the United States of America

The Virginia Convention of 1829-30.

A DISCOURSE

DELIVERED BEFORE

THE VIRGINIA HISTORICAL SOCIETY.

AT THEIR

ANNUAL MEETING,

Held in the Athenaeum in the City of Richmond,

DECEMBER 15TH, 1853.

BY HUGH B. GRIGSBY.

PUBLISHED BY THE SOCIETY.

RICHMOND:
MACFARLANE & FERGUSSON.
1854.

DISCURSE.

Mr. President and Gentlemen
of the Virginia Historical Society:

Could we point to some succinct and authentic record of
the lives of those great men who laid the foundations of
our institutions and reared upon them the structure, which
it was the privilege of our fathers and ourselves for half a
century to inhabit,—how delightful would be the office of
pointing out their worth to the young men of the country,
and of exhorting them to imitate their glorious example?
Alas! no such record exists; and the Virginian, old and
young, knows less of George Mason and Edmund Pendleton, than he does of the statesmen of Greece or Rome;
and when the patriotic parent is sensible of the importance
of imbuing the youthful mind with a knowledge of our
early benefactors, he finds the task difficult and almost impossible. Much has been lost, but much may yet be done.
I hold that every fact relating to those eminent men is of
real value. It may seem at first immaterial to know that
Pendleton was a cripple; but, when it is known that, lame
as he was, and unable to rise from his chair to put a question to the house, he was nevertheless unanimously chosen
president of the Virginia Convention of 1788, and allowed
to perform the duties of the station sitting, and afterwards
presided for so many years in our highest courts, the fact
contains a moral which posterity will delight to learn and
to apply. Let us hope that the glory of performing such

an office awaits some member of our association, and, if he should execute it with the skill and grace with which the character and services of Hampden have been recorded by an eminent Virginian, he will accomplish a work which the present age will hail with applause, and which posterity, if I may use the words of Milton just quoted by the chair, will not willingly let die.

I come to lay my own humble but grateful tribute at the shrine of the past, and, while I sincerely wish that the task of recalling to the recollection of the present generation the lives and services of the members of the Virginia Convention of 1829-30 had been assigned to worthier hands than mine, I trust the readiness with which I have undertaken it, deeply sensible as I am of its difficulty and delicacy, will afford no uncertain measure of the regard with which I cherish the purposes of our society, and of my thorough conviction of its importance to the historical literature of our native State. Premising that I shall mainly speak of those members who are no longer living, with a becoming respect to their memory indeed, but with all the freedom of history, I proceed at once to my office.

When the General Assembly of Virginia, during the winter of 1828-9, passed the act calling a Convention, to be composed of four delegates from each senatorial district, and required it to assemble in the city of Richmond on the fifth of October following, the attention of the people was soon directed to the choice of delegates to so important a body. Federal politics were laid aside ; and public worth and eminent abilities were the only standards in the selection of its members. Actual residence was overlooked, and the unusual sight was presented of one district selecting its representatives from another and a distant one. What was rarer still, the opinions of many of persons voted for were unknown, and in a comparatively few instances did any candidate address the people from the hustings.

A body of men, selected under such circumstances, might well attract attention at home and abroad ; and the period of its assembling drew towards Richmond a large concourse of intelligent persons from various parts of the Union. Young men came on horseback from Kentucky, Tennessee, and other Southern States. Statesmen, men of mature years, who had already earned for themselves a title to the public regard, ministers of foreign powers, who wished to see men whose names had become historical, educated men of every profession and class, came, many of them with their families, to behold the gathering, and listen to the discussions of the body. The citizens of Virginia, who came to Richmond from within her own borders and from abroad, would alone have formed an auditory, which any speaker would have been proud to address.

It was about ten o'clock of the fifth of October, 1829, a morning as lovely and as auspicious as could have been chosen, that hundreds of persons, of all ages, were seen thronging the public square, and walking through the apartments of the Capitol, now halting about the statue of Washington, which was soon to look down on some of the patriots and sages who had upheld the living original in the field and in the cabinet, then moving towards the library, then recently established, which was thrown open to public inspection. As the hour of twelve drew near, and the members elect began to assemble in the hall of the House of Delegates, and exchange salutations, the crowd gravitated toward the gallery and the lobby, and filled every place from which it was possible to see or hear. At twelve, the house was called to order by JAMES MADISON, who nominated JAMES MONROE as President of the Convention, and was seconded by JOHN MARSHALL. That the nomination

100585

of such a man, made by such men, was unanimously con-
firmed, is known to all.

Here let us pause, and contemplate the members who
then filled the seats in that hall. To behold those venerable men—to listen to their names as they fell distinctly and
deliberately from the lips of the accomplished clerk, was
to feel the whole history of Virginia from the memorable
session of 1765 to that moment flash full upon you.
It is true, that no member of the House of Burgesses of
1765 was present, nor any one, who, like the youthful Jefferson, had heard the eloquence of Henry in defence of
his resolutions. Peyton Randolph had departed before the
clouds had begun to break away from the sky of the Revolution. The waters of the Potomac and the Staunton had
been flowing beside the graves of Washington and Henry
for more than a quarter of a century; and before Washington and Henry had departed, Richard Henry Lee had
been gathered to his fathers amid the shades of Chantilly.
It was the fortune of George Wythe and Edmund Pendleton to survive to the present century, and to behold the
federal government in the full tide of successful experi-
ment, their ancient friend, Thomas Jefferson, at the helm.
Paul Carrington, who had moved the appointment of Peyton Randolph as President of the Convention of 1775, and
of Edmund Pendleton as President of the Convention of
1788, and was the last survivor of the House of Burgesses
of 1765, had died eleven years before. The author of the
Declaration of Independence, who, as a spectator in the
lobby, had drank in the inspiration of Henry's eloquence
in the debate on the resolutions against the stamp act, and
has given us the most interesting reminiscences of the
scene, had died in less than four years before the meeting
of the body. These distinguished patriots were not indeed
present in the Convention of 1829-30, yet were so con-

nected in their lives with those who were, that our whole
history seemed reflected in the panorama that was moving
before us. If Jefferson were not present, there was Madison, who carried out in the Assembly the great measures
which his absence during his mission to the Court of
France rendered it impracticable for him to do in person,
and to whom he had recently said: "To myself you have
been a pillar of support through life; take care of me
when dead." If Pendleton and Wythe did not appear,
there were Madison and Marshall, who had struggled with
them in the Convention of 1788 against the eloquence of
Henry, and who brought them into view; and if Grayson
and George Mason were absent, there was Monroe, who
united with them in opposing the adoption of the federal
constitution by the people of Virginia. Marshall and Monroe had been with Washington in some of the hard contested fields of the Revolution, while Madison in the councils of Virginia, and in the Congress of the Confederation,
had sustained by his eloquence and patriotism the plans of
our Great Leader. If George Mason, who drafted the
constitution which the Convention was assembled to revise, was no more, there was Madison who aided him in
sustaining that instrument in the Convention of 1776, and
who could speak in his behalf.

Perhaps the most important act in our history was the
adoption of the federal constitution,—an act, the full pur-
port of which was not known at the time of its adoption,
if indeed it is fully known at present; and the history of
that instrument and of the measures of those who carried
it into execution, was wrapped up in the lives of the men
who then sat in that hall. If to any one individual more
than another the paternity of the federal constitution may
be ascribed, James Madison was that man. It may be that
the present form of that paper is from the pen of Gouver-

neur Morris, but Madison was the inspiring genius of the
new system. He it was, who, while a member of the old
Congress, drew the celebrated appeal to the people at the
close of the war to adopt some efficient mode of paying
the debts of the confederation ; who procured in 1786 the
passage of the resolution of this commonwealth inviting
the meeting at Annapolis, which resulted in the assembling
of the Convention in Philadelphia ; who attended the sessions of that body, and as much as any one man, if not
more, guided its deliberations. He, too, was the author of
the letter accompanying the constitution, signed by Washington, and addressed to the President of Congress. He
it was, who with Jay and Hamilton sustained the constitution by those essays which, under the name of the Federalist, have attained the dignity of a text-book and a classic. He it was who, more than any one man, braced the
nerves of the Virginia Convention of 1788, while Henry,
George Mason, Grayson and Monroe were breathing awful
imprecations on the head of the new system ; and who
drafted the form of ratification of that instrument by the
body ;—a form destined to be known better hereafter than
it is at present. He it was, who repaired to New York,
and assisted in the deliberations of the first Congress. He
it was, whose influence was felt in the federal councils,
either by his personal presence as a member of the House
of Representatives, Secretary of State, and President, or
by his writings from 1786, when Virginia adopted his resolution inviting the meeting at Annapolis, to the moment
of the assembling of the body of which he was then a
member. The history of that one man was the history of
his country. There, to the extreme left of the chair, as it
then stood, dressed in black, with an olive colored over-
coat, now and then raising his hand to his powdered hair,

and studiously attentive to every speaker, he was sitting before you.

When Mr. Madison took his seat in the Convention, he was in the seventy-ninth year of his age; yet, though so far advanced in life, and entitled alike by age and position to ease, he attended the meetings of the body during a session of three months and a half without the loss, so far as I now remember, of more than a single day. That he was entitled to the chair, and that the universal expectation was that he should receive that honor, none knew better, or could have acknowledged more gracefully, than did Mr. Monroe. He spoke but two or three times, when he ascertained that his voice was too low to be heard; possibly, too, he might have been averse from mingling too closely in the bitter strifes of a new generation. When he rose to speak, the members, old as well as young, left their seats, and, like children about to receive the words of wisdom from the lips of an aged father, gathered around him. That he still retained the vigor of his intellect, and that unapproachable grace in his written compositions, his two short speeches written out by himself, and his letters to Mr. Cabell, Mr. Everett, and Mr. Ingersoll on the Tariff, Bank and Nullification controversies, show clearly enough.

As a speaker, Mr. Madison was more distinguished by intellectual than physical qualities. His voice at no period of his life was strong enough to be heard distinctly in a large assembly. In the House of Delegates of which he was a member at intervals from 1776 to 1788, and in 1799, his influence in debate was more by the impression which he made upon prominent men than upon the house itself. The Continental Congress and the Philadelphia federal convention, in which he gained so much renown, were small bodies, rarely exceeding forty, and sometimes not half that number, and were within the range of his voice.

The first Congress under the federal constitution was composed of less than sixty members, Rhode Island and North Carolina not having then adopted that instrument, and its whole complement was but sixty-five. But in the Virginia federal convention and in the House of Delegates, the numbers of which exceeded those of the two bodies first named four times, and of the last named nearly three times, he was rarely heard throughout the hall. Several of the finest passages in his speeches in the Virginia federal convention are lost to posterity from the weakness of his voice.

His style of debate was in unison with his general character, and partook more of the essay than the speech. He adhered closely to his subject, and, avoiding all personalities towards others, was prompt, however, to repel them when aimed at himself. When Grayson, in the convention of '88, made some allusions to him of a personal nature, he instantly rose and demanded an unequivocal retraction. This was the only instance of a personal kind that he encountered during the session, and, perhaps, throughout his whole career, while Patrick Henry and Edmund Randolph, who had been friends, became, in the course of the session, bitter enemies; and it is probable that the amicable relations of George Nicholas and Henry were seriously impaired by the collisions of debate.

It would be difficult to estimate too highly his services in the Virginia federal convention. As he had studied the Constitution as a whole, which no other member except George Mason had done, and discussed it minutely in the numbers of the Federalist; moreover, as he had been one of the most active members of the body which formed it, he stood by its side throughout the session of twenty-five days, and explained its probable working as readily as if he had seen it in full operation for a quarter of a century. It required his ready tact, his range of historical illustration, and his philosophical caste of mind which kept him free from the personalities of debate, to reassure the friends of the constitution, who were daily shaken by the vaticinations of Henry and Mason, and to reconcile them to its adoption. As it was, in a house of one hundred and sixty-eight members, it was carried by a majority of ten votes only. When it is remembered that the favorable vote of Virginia was alone wanting to save the constitution, eight States having already ratified it, and that North Carolina and Rhode Island afterwards refused to adopt it, it is more than probable that its rejection by the largest State in the confederation, as Virginia then was, would have settled its fate, and the federal constitution would have sunk to rise no more. If the adoption of that system were wise and proper;—if it has shed boundless blessings on our own people, and lifted its cheering light to the eyes of the oppressed of every clime; and if such a glorious result can be traced to the action of any one State and any one man, VIRGINIA is the State, and JAMES MADISON is the man, to whom honor is due.

I have said that Mr. Madison rarely took part in the proceedings of the Convention then sitting. It was in conversation that he made the strongest impression on the hearts of all who sought him. A severe student in early life, he never forsook his first love, and the accuracy and freshness of his literary and political reminiscences astonished the admiring listener. In the midst of his retirement he had watched the general current of history, and was prompt to correct any material error. His graceful refutation of a theory of the historian Robertson, which he presented in the course of an agricultural address in 1819, is well known; and when Dr. Ramsay, in his account of the Revolution, alluded to the instructions of Virginia to her delegates in the Continental Congress, on the subject

of a surrender of the navigation of the Mississippi, in such
a way as to conflict with the consistency of the State, he
stepped forth and put the whole subject in its proper light.
Whatever he did, was thoroughly done. The memorial on
religious freedom prepared by him in 1780, in which he
demonstrated, perhaps for the first time, the cardinal doctrines which ought to control governments in matters of
religion, was mainly efficient in putting an end to that un-
natural connexion between church and state to which some
of the ablest statesmen of the Revolution, guided by early
prejudice, too closely adhered, and will henceforth appear,
as well from the beauty of its style as from the weight of
its philosophy, among the most conspicuous religious landmarks in the history of our race.   He was the delight of
the social circle, and seemed incapable of imputing a harsh
motive to any human being ; and to a young friend, fresh
from a New England College, he spoke of Quincy, Otis,
Daggett, Dexter, and the younger Sherman,—men who had
opposed his administration with a zeal that brought them
to the verge of disunion—with as deliberate an appreciation of their merits as if they had held a far different
course. But he preferred to dwell on incidents of an earlier period, and recalled to his young friends in his charm-
ing way the memory of Witherspoon who blended so intimately the duties of the scholar and the statesman, and
who was the guide of his youth,—of Franklin, and of the
elder Sherman, with both of whom he had been intimate
in early life.   His wife, whose elegance diffused a lustre
over his public career, and who was the light of his rural
home, accompanied him to Richmond, and, as you left
their presence, it was impossible not to rejoice that Provi-
dence had allotted to such a couple an old age so lovely.

But, prominent as was Mr. Madison in that Convention,
none would allow sooner than he that he was among equals.

No individual could vie with him in his peculiar career in federal politics, nor in that happy combination of faculties, which, comprehending all classes of political subjects, had adorned them all. In general learning he was not only ahead of his contemporaries in that body, but may be said to have stood alone. Not even the raciness and research of Mr. Jefferson could surpass him; and if he had devoted his time to jurisprudence, the student would not have been compelled, if he did not recognise them in Story, to look abroad for the blended strength and elegance of a Stowell. But there were men now before him, whose career was contemporaneous with his own, as well as others who had grown into eminence since the beginning of the century, who had shared or might well have shared divided empire with him. In surveying a body of men, the representatives of two generations, the observer, with a view of arranging them in their respective classes, would insensibly call to mind the leading epochs in the two great parties of the country, since the adoption of the federal constitution This period, at least for the present purpose, readily resolves itself into four great epochs; the first extending from the organization of the government in 1789 to the close of the administration of the elder Adams; the second, from 1801 to the year 1806, when the restrictive policy of the administration made a breach in the ranks of the republican party; the third from 1806 to the close of the war in 1815; and the fourth from 1815 to the assembling of the Convention. Now of these important epochs the most influential personages were assembled in that hall.

Of the first epoch—from 1789 to 1801, there were Madison, Monroe, Marshall, Giles, Randolph, Taliaferro and Tazewell. The history of these names is the history of the period. Madison and Giles in the House of Representatives, and Monroe in the Senate, guided the counsels

of one great party, until the two first in 1798, retired with
a view of entering the General Assembly, and the last
was sent as envoy to the French republic. Their influence in their new spheres is known to all. Randolph did
not enter the House of Representatives till 1799, and Tazewell, who had voted with Madison and Giles in the memorable session of the Assembly in 1799, and was elected to
fill the vacancy made by the appointment of Judge Marshall to the War Department, did not take his seat till 1800.

Here we approach one of those monumental names which
make the era in which they appear their own. What Edmund Randolph said of himself is quite as applicable to
John Marshall,—that he was a child of the Revolution. He
had seen the first flash of the war at the Great Bridge, had
been at Brandywine, Germantown, and Monmouth, and
had gone forth under Steuben. In 1782 began his legal
and political career; and from that time till 1796, he was
at intervals a member of the House of Delegates. Here
he won some of his greenest laurels. In the Virginia convention of 1788, he made a speech which called forth the
praise of Madison. It was near the close of this epoch he
entered the House of Representatives, and, although he
remained but one session, and made but one regular speech,
he gained great distinction, and was regarded as the leader
of the administration of Adams in the Southern States.
He had fought the battles of his party with such success
in the House of Delegates, and had inspired such confidence in his patriotism and purity of purpose, that the lof-
tiest honors of the Washington and Adams' administrations
were within his reach. Washington solicited him to accept
the office of Attorney General and the mission to France;
but he declined both; and it was only at the urgent solici-
tation of the greatest names that he consented at a later
period to accept the French mission. From the War he

passed to the State Department, and thence, in 1800, to
the office of Chief Justice, which he filled until his de-
cease in 1835, a space of more than thirty five years, during which he was the judicial arbiter of his country. This
is not the place to review his judicial career; but it may
be said, that it was his singular glory that, though called
from the fiercest political contests to decide questions which
have been and are the themes of party discord, and concerning which there has been and will ever be a difference
of opinion, he has not only escaped any serious suspicion
of improper bias, but, by the supremacy of his genius and
the simple majesty of his deportment, won the general admiration and regard.

The personal appearance of Judge Marshall, and his
manner of speaking, will be known to posterity from the
descriptions of Wirt, and the British Spy is in every hand.
He spoke but seldom in the Convention, and always with
deliberation. I would say that an intense earnestness was
the leading trait of his manner. His first speech was made
at a time when a spirit of compromise began to shew itself.
When he had demonstrated conclusively that the federal
basis was the mean proportional between the two extremes
of the bases which had engaged the public attention, he
examined with critical care the schemes which had been
offered, and exhibited by way of comparison some calcu-
lations of his own. He bore his testimony in favor of the
County Court system, and defended it briefly but ably. It
was in the discussion of the judicial tenure, that he came
forth in all his strength. The question was virtually the
same as that presented in Congress in 1802 on the repeal
of the judiciary act; and what enhanced the interest of
the debate, was the presence of Mr. Randolph, who reported the bill to repeal the judiciary act of 1800, and of Mr.
Giles who had advocated the repeal in the House of Rep-

resentatives, and both of whom engaged in the present debate.   He spoke with deep feeling, and, though pressed by
Tazewell, Giles, and Barbour of Orange, he maintained his
ground with surpassing skill ; and when in conclusion, and
under the full excitement of debate, he declared : "I have
always thought from my earliest youth till now, that the
greatest curse an angry heaven ever inflicted upon an un-
grateful and a sinning people, was an ignorant, a corrupt,
or a dependent judiciary.   Will you call down this curse
on Virginia ?" all felt the power of his eloquence.   Let me
observe that the debate on the tenure of the judicial office—
a debate in which Marshall, Tazewell, Leigh, Scott, Jon-
son, Giles, Randolph, and Barbour of Orange, engaged ;—
was one of the most brilliant exhibitions of the Convention.

In the domestic relations of life, which, as they ever afford the true test of intrinsic worth, become the crowning
grace of an illustrious character, he was beyond all praise.
Great in intellect he undoubtedly was, but he was as good
as he was great ; and those who knew him longest and
best, found it hard to say whether they regarded him most
with veneration or love.

But, however eminent as a debater, a statesman, and a
jurist, it is in the garb of an historian that he will appear
most frequently before the generations to come, and it is
the only garb that sets ungracefully upon him.   The life of
Washington, if I may so speak, was made to order.   The
federal party was fast melting away.   The administration
of Jefferson was in the full tide of success.   The alien law
had expired by its own limitation.   The sedition law had
also expired, and its victims were set free.   The judiciary
act had been swept from the statute-book.   The charter of
the Bank of the United States and the assumption act
were in bad odor, and would have been repealed, if it had

been practicable. The excise law was numbered with the slain. Every vestige of the past dynasty was disappearing. A new generation, which partook of the opinions around it, was stepping on the stage. Now was the time for a master spirit to appear, who might not only recover the lost ground, but gain fresh conquests. Politicians of both parties had long known the abilities of John Marshall. He had broken the force of many a democratic measure in the House of Delegates. In the convention of 1788, he seized with great tact the phantoms which the genius of Henry had raised, reduced them to substantial forms, and broke them on the wheel of his resistless logic. His correspondence with the French Directory, and especially the celebrated letter to the Minister of Foreign Affairs, almost a book in itself, which, though signed by Gerry and Cotesworth Pinckney, was from his pen, and which was not only unanswered but unanswerable, had been published in all the papers, and was universally applauded. His speech in the case of Jonathan Robbins, which was his first great effort in the House of Representatives, into which he entered soon after his return from France, raised his reputation still higher in the estimation alike of friends and opponents. And it was hoped that a history from his hand of the federal party during the administration of Washington, and under the wing of his great name, would make a deep impression on the popular mind. But to be effectual it must come forth at once. The most courteous republican was not bound to wait for it. A princely sum, then unknown in the annals of American authorship, awaited its completion. And in due time, and in five volumes, it made its appearance. Mr. Jefferson was in the second year of his second term. He had been re-elected almost without opposition. There was hardly a show of fight at the polls. To put down the doctrines of the party

of which he was the head was the mission of the new
book ; and, by a singular coincidence, simultaneously with
the appearance of the book, occurred the schism in the
republican party on the restrictive policy of the administration.   Still it came too late.

From the data already given, and with a knowledge of
the fact that the author was engaged in performing official
duties arduous enough to employ the time and all the faculties of ordinary men, a literary geometer might have de.
scribed beforehand its essential form and character.   Of
all the kinds of writing that of history is most difficult.
A great speech, a well-reasoned State paper, a fine poem,
may be struck off from the impulse, or under the inspiration, of the moment; but to write history requires other
and more complicated qualifications; qualifications which
cannot be conjured up for the nonce, and which are so
rare, that, while the number of histories is legion, the
names of the great historians, like those of the great epic
poets, may be written in a nutshell.   Probably, when Marshall undertook the composition of his work, he had never
contemplated with critical accuracy the distinctive merits
of any great history.   His early opportunities of acquiring
knowledge were few ; and, instead of spending his youth
and middle age in the closet with Hume and Gibbon, cull-
ing phrases and recasting periods, he was engaged in the
field contending for the liberties of his country, or in the
busy strifes of the bar in pursuit of an honorable independence.   But this explanation, while it accounts for the absence of those qualities which make an excellent history,
by no means supplies the defect.   The result is, that the
Life of Washington—I speak of the fifth and leading volume of the first edition—is a strong off-hand argument in
defence of the measures of the federal party during the
administration of Washington, and, if it had been pronoun-

ced in the House of Delegates, or in the House of Representatives, it would have passed well enough, and only be-
comes out of place when put into the mouth of the muse
of history. As might fairly have been anticipated, a work
from such a hand, though it was not to make a revolution
in existing parties, produced a marked effect. Of its strictly
literary merits, there was at home and abroad but one
opinion; but, while the political friends of the author hailed
its appearance with joy, and were quite willing to shelter
themselves behind the massy bulwark which it reared in
their defence, it was warmly condemned by the opposite
party. Mr. Jefferson protested against it to the end of his
life, and died in the full belief that Mr. Madison was pre-
paring a counter-history, or at least a refutation of the
fifth volume. Mr. Giles, at a late day, addressed a letter
to the author, disclaiming certain expressions attributed to
him, but not materially objecting, if I remember rightly,
to their substantial meaning. It is proper to say that the
second edition presents the work in a greatly amended
form. The colonial history is separated from the body of
the work, and has been revised with great care and respect
for authorities then accessible. The style of the work is
greatly improved in the new edition. Not only are the
grammatical errors corrected, but the diction approaches to
purity and sometimes to elegance. In a note to the second
volume of the second edition, he examines at length the
charges of Mr. Jefferson on the subject of the Mazzei letter, but does not allude to other objections urged by him
against the work. From the blended influence of the names
of Washington and Marshall, the history in its new form
will always hold a place in our libraries, but it may be allowed the mere student of history as well as the statesman and the politician to regret that a history of the same

epoch from the pen of Madison does not exist to take its station by its side.

No two eminent contemporaries appear at the first glance to have fewer points of friendly contact and connexion, if not of resemblance, than James Madison and John Marshall. In their persons, dress, manners and mind, they appear to be in strong contrast. Madison, from infancy to age, was of a delicate constitution, small in stature, scrupulously attentive to his dress, and, though accessible and easy of approach, and in the highest degree courteous, was, like most delicate men, naturally reserved. Marshall enjoyed robust health in his early years, was six feet high, was ordinarily regardless of his personal appearance, and was hearty in his address, retaining to the last the downright cordiality of the camp. Madison was extremely social in his feelings, but these were exhibited in his parlour from the walls of which the works of the first masters of painting were looking down upon him, or in his library in the midst of his cherished books, with far more zest than under the freshening influences of physical exertion. If he sought exercise, it was on a well-broken horse, or from a drive in his carriage. He had no taste or strength for the rougher modes of muscular exertion. Marshall never lost his youthful habits of early rising, of walks over hill and moor, which he had taken with a musket on his shoulder and a knapsack on his back at the darkest hour of the Revolution, and of contests of personal strength. He would enjoy with as much relish a triumph on the quoit ground as at the bar, or on the bench. If Madison had lived in a city, he would have despatched every morning to market a well-dressed servant, with a tidy basket on his arm, and supplied his table through him. Marshall did his own marketing, and not unfrequently brought it home with his own hands. The grounds of Madison's town-residence would have exhibited a specimen of landscape gardening, and a view *in petto* of the Virginian Flora. Marshall, like Stephen Girard, had no opinion of a plant or a tree that did not bear something for the support of human life ; and would have had a bed of fine cabbages or an orchard of delicious fruit. Madison spent his youth at Nassau Hall, as a student and resident graduate. Marshall had few opportunities of acquiring knowledge in his boyhood, and was engaged in the labors of the farm. Madison, who was four years older than Marshall, chose the cabinet; Marshall took the battlefield and the bar. These diversities lie on the surface, and strike the attention at once. Yet it will appear that there were points of friendly contact and communion between these eminent men from the beginning to the end of their lives. Both were members of the House of Delegates prior to 1788, and exerted their influence to provide for the debt of the Revolution, and to amend the articles of confederation. When the federal constitution was formed, Madison and Marshall were among the ablest champions in sustaining it before the people. And when the Virginia federal convention was assembled, on Madison and Marshall, as much, if not more than on any other two men, did the responsibility of defending that instrument devolve. In the organization of the new government they went hand in hand. Both enjoyed the unlimited confidence of Washington, and could have obtained the honor of a seat in his cabinet. Marshall went to France in 1797, but Madison had previously declined a mission to the same court. Both filled the office of Secretary of State at the most trying periods of our foreign relations, and acquitted themselves with equal honor. Marshall was called to the highest seat in the federal judiciary, and Madison to the highest seat in the federal executive ; yet the questions which engaged the attention of each, from the perplexed commercial relations of the period, were nearly the same. The famous tract of Stephen, "War in Disguise," was as closely studied by Marshall as by Madison ; and, if Madison, as a politician, was required to refute it through the press, Marshall, as a judge, was compelled to examine its doctrines on the bench. From the commercial difficulties which existed from 1800, when Marshall took his seat on the bench, to 1817, when Madison retired from the Presidency, the number of topics' of common interest between the Executive and Judiciary departments of government was greater than it has been since, or will be again, unless it shall be our misfortune to see all Europe at loggerheads, and to be involved in a quasi-war with the two greatest commercial nations of the globe. These eminent men moved in different orbits, but were bound by a common law and a common sympathy. Both possessed minds of the highest order—*magis pares quam similes*—and peculiarly adapted to their respective spheres. Both were distinguished for their generous humanity, the strength of their friendships, and the moral beauty of their lives. And, fortunately, both were summoned by their country to afford their aid in revising the constitution of their native State ; and here—in this city—where it had begun fifty years before, and which had been uninterrupted by a solitary act or word of unkindness toward each other, both closed their long and illustrious political career.

Among the names of this epoch which demand something more than a passing notice, is that of WILLIAM BRANCH GILES. He had taken his degree at Nassau Hall in 1781, ten years after Madison had taken his at the same college, and had the good fortune also of receiving the instructions of Witherspoon, whose memory in familiar talk with his younger friends he delighted even in old age to recall. A member of the House of Representatives from

1790 to 1798, and from 1800 to 1803, and of the Senate of the United States from 1804 to 1815, he was beyond any other man the great champion of his party in public debate. That he performed his part successfully may be inferred from the fact that Mr. Jefferson pronounced him the ablest debater of the age. He was then the Governor of Virginia. In all things but in the vigor of his intellect, he was but the shadow of his former self. He could neither move nor stand without the aid of his crutches, and, when on the conclusion of his able speech on the basis question, the members pressed their congratulations upon him, he seemed to belong rather to the dead than the living. His face was the face of a corpse. Although he was four years younger than Monroe, seven younger than Marshall, and eleven younger than Madison, his personal appearance had suffered more from disease than that of any of his early contemporaries. To behold his rugged face and beetling brows, such as are now preserved in the portrait by Ford, it was difficult to believe that he was the handsome young man, radiant with health and arrayed in the rich costume of the last century, that is represented in one of the finest portraits from the easel of Stuart.

He was strongly attached to the existing constitution, which he had defended in one of his ablest speeches two years before in the House of Delegates, and he evidently came to speak on the basis question with his life in his hand. To criticize the action of a dying man would be idle enough; yet it was plain to see what were the characteristics of his manner in his prime. His mode of speaking was conversational. His political illustrations were mainly drawn from the British constitution, and from the federal government, in the service of which so much of his life was spent. His range of reading beyond the common walks of history did not appear extensive, and it was obvious that he had paid but slight attention to the ornamental departments of literature. His comparisons were usually drawn from common life, and before a Virginia audience he was irresistible. He had practised law with success four or five years before he entered the House of Representatives, and was always able, with some preparation, to cope on legal topics with his ablest opponents. In his speech in the Convention on the judicial tenure, to which an allusion has already been made, he showed that he had not forgotten the excitements of a time long gone by, and gave to his auditors the best specimen which they had yet seen, of those powers of debate for which he was so justly renowned. It was his wish to speak on the subject of corporations, and he had prepared himself carefully for the occasion, but, his increasing infirmities confining him almost constantly to his room, his resolutions were definitively acted upon during his absence. His published writings, though revised by himself, will afford posterity an imperfect standard in estimating his powers in debate.

To those who are fascinated with the glitter of a public career the life of Mr. Giles presents a striking lesson. He had fought all the great battles of his party, many of them single handed, against the greatest odds and always with success, and borne the brunt of the fight from 1790 to his retirement in 1815 from the Senate of the United States. He had defended the Report of 1799 in the House of Delegates, and was mainly relied upon to withstand the force of Patrick Henry, who had been elected to the Assembly, but died before its meeting. He had more than any other individual, not excepting Mr. Madison, sustained the doctrines of his party in the House of Representatives and in the Senate, and was thoroughly committed to all its great measures. He had fought through the darkness of a long and cheerless night to the dawn of day, and just as the day was breaking, and he felt that he might at length repose safely upon his well-earned laurels, a storm suddenly rose that was to sweep them from his brow.

The session of the General Assembly of 1811-12 presented a crisis in the history of parties. Issues that had been ringing for six years past in the public ear had suddenly died away. Non-intercourse and embargo were no longer talked of. The war, which was to sink them forever, and to cover the country with a blaze of glory, had not yet been declared. For the first time since 1806, the republicans, so called, had recently received the aid of their dissenting brethren. The constitutionality of a Bank of the United States had brought them together at the preceding session. But in the interval Mr. Giles had expressed some opinions in the Senate on the right of instruction, which were not in unison with those of his party, but had declared in the strongest terms his readiness to obey the instructions of the Assembly, and to carry out to the utmost all its wishes. As he was the oldest public servant in Congress, and had borne aloft the ark of the political covenant at a stormy period, when most of those who were about to instruct him were in their swaddling clothes or in the first forms of the schools: as he had ever been prompt in the discharge of the most difficult and perplexing offices of party, and had clung to the laboring oar while his compatriots had once and again sought the honor and profit of a foreign mission, or a seat in one of the departments or on the bench, or tasted the fruits of service in retirement, it would seem that a distinct affirmation of the principles of the Assembly, and an expression of its regret at the difference of opinion on this isolated question, coupled with an honorable recognition of the great services of Mr. Giles, were all that the occasion demanded. And in ordinary times such probably would have been the case. But such a policy was not suited to the mood of the moment. It was a remarkable era of political fusion. Men, who had long eyed one another askance in the House of Delegates, now shook hands, inquired every morning after each other's health, and laughed immoderately at each other's jokes. The lunch and the dinner were potent weapons of the day. Cobwebs woven during the consulship of Plancus—*consule Planco*—were hurriedly brushed aside, and the long-imprisoned juice once more sparkled. in the face of day. There was a commingling of old friends and old enemies, of federalists and republicans, and of that vigorous offshoot of one party, and the active ally of the other, the *tertium quids.* To bind together such a brotherhood two things were indispensable ; a common ground to stand on, and a common victim. The first was found in the right of the Assembly to instruct the representatives of Virginia in the Senate of the United States, and the victim was found in the person of Mr. Giles. A more fortunate selection of a victim could not have been made. To the tertium quids, who once loved him and hated him the more,—whose schemes he had ever been the first to detect and the strongest to crush,—he was thoroughly odious; he could not be more so than he was ; and these enemies had become the eager allies of his friends. The federalists, who never loved him and who hated him the less, but from whom of all men living he had the least to hope, delighted at the prospect of beholding the sacrifice of their most formidable foe by his own friends, clapped their hands and shouted Io Pæan in the ecstasy of their joy. It was easy for the new brotherhood, under the influence of good dinners and old wine, to chat pleasantly of former times, to grow very loving, and insensibly to glide together to some half-way house in the past. It is a noteworthy fact in political ethics, that parties, when the danger is past, are too apt to sacrifice soon-

est those who were most prominent in defence of measures
deemed vital at the time, but which in the retrospect appear of doubtful policy.   Mr. Giles, two or three years before, had brought in a bill to define treason, defended it in
a speech, and carried it through the Senate.   He had also
brought in a bill to suspend the writ of *habeas corpus*, sustained it in a speech, and carried it through the Senate.
Unwise and dangerous measures these may have been at
any time, but, when discussed over a glass of wine in a
season of comparative tranquility, they were absolutely
shocking.   Still they were called for by a republican administration, and were upheld by its friends at a time when
condemnation, if ever, was justly due.   These bills were
defeated in the House of Representatives.   Here was
another fact for the new brotherhood.   It separated the
republicans of the House from those of the Senate ; and,
if a Senator were sacrificed, the act might not only not
reflect injuriously on the members of the House, but might
imply an appreciation of their conduct.   I do not affirm
that these were the ostensible grounds of difficulty between
Mr. Giles and the Assembly, nor is this the place to detail
at length the controversy which ensued ; but whoever will
look into the secret history of that day will be apt to con-
clude, that the torch which was applied to the funeral pile
of Giles was lighted at a fire kindled some years before for
the sacrifice of a still more illustrious personage.   The result was that Mr. Giles came to the ground with a force
unknown in the annals of political tumbling.   From a
height of popularity almost unequalled he became the
most unpopular man in the State.   He lingered in the
Senate until the beginning of 1815, when he withdrew to
the Wigwam.   Years rolled on.   A retributive ray of the
public sunshine was at last seen to play about his hoary
temples, and to cheer his brave old heart.   He lived to be

elected Governor thrice by a republican Assembly, and to gain distinction in a new sphere; but he did not live to see that mighty master-spirit, now sitting near him, who pressed the bitter cup to his lips, receive it on his own.

The second great epoch extending from the accession of Mr. Jefferson in 1801 to the second term of his administration in 1806, was fully represented in that body. Madison, whose nomination to the Senate had been defeated by Patrick Henry, and who had hitherto appeared in the House of Representatives only, now bore on his shoulders the burden in no wise light of the State department. In the Senate Mr. Giles sustained the administration with increasing fame, while Monroe, who had exchanged his seat in the Senate for the mission to England, brought his untiring industry and zeal to bear in the same cause abroad. Randolph and James Mercer Garnett, who were now in the House of Representatives, and Tazewell, who, unless when sent to the Assembly on some occasion of special interest to the people of Norfolk with whom he had now taken up his abode, was in private life, were toward the close of the term ranged in the opposition. Randolph had taken his seat in the House of Representatives in 1799, with but slight preparation for the new career he was about to begin. I am not aware that he ever spoke in public before he entered Congress. It is true that he was a candidate for Congress, when Patrick Henry, who was a candidate for a seat in the House of Delegates, made at the March court before the election from the porch of the old tavern at Charlotte Court House his last address to the people, but, having a severe cold, he was able to say a few words only; and all reports to the contrary must be ranked among those kindly myths which popular tradition delights to strew over the cradle of genius. He soon, however, attracted public attention by his fearlessness of spirit, and by the point and

brilliancy of his speeches in the house, and had now attained the responsible and laborious position at the head of
the committee of ways and means. Thus far he had sailed
with the administration. He had labored in the cause of
retrenchment and reform with such indefatigable industry
as seriously to impair his sight. He had made in his speech
on the judiciary repeal bill by far his most brilliant display,
and had heartily approved the purchase of Louisiana;—a
measure which he then saw in all its present usefulness,
and in all its glorious promise. From this date he declared
unceasing war against his former friends. He well knew
that the great party from which he was about to separate
himself, guided by ancient associations, was disposed to
regard France with kinder feelings than it did England,
and he accordingly sought to put in train a course of measures which would involve the country in a war with Spain,
which necessarily involved a war with France. He opposed with warmth the restrictive policy of the administration, and in later life he has been heard to say, that " when
Mr. Jefferson made war upon his tobacco, he made war
upon him ;" and, as he is reported to have said, that his estate, when it came into his possession, was mortgaged nine-
teen shillings and six pence in the pound, it is quite certain
that a policy which checked the free interchange of com-
modities with foreign nations, would prove most hostile to
his private interests. Contemporaneously, however, with
his hostility to the party of which heretofore he had been
a prominent member, was the appointment of a Minister
to the Court of St. James, and it was rumored that private
griefs were mixed up with his politics. That such a charge
was generally believed at that day is certain, and that the
administration believed that he desired the mission to England and declined to confer it upon him, is a fact which
seems to rest on unquestionable testimony. Whether Mr.

Randolph was privy to any action in the premises, is another and a very different question. There, sitting within a few feet of him, was the man who could settle the question at once. Yet let those who are inclined to think that personal feelings impelled Mr. Randolph in his new career, reflect upon his elevated position, and what it was to oppose such a man as Mr. Jefferson. I have already alluded to the exalted position of Mr. Randolph in the House of Representatives, and before the country. If we were to judge of the popularity of Mr. Jefferson by the standard which we apply to modern Presidents, we would err widely. It was far-reaching and overwhelming. Nothing equal to it had been seen before ; nothing equal to it has been seen since ; and nothing equal to it will, I trust, be seen again. Such was the fascinating address of that illustrious man, such the high estimate of his services abroad and at home, so universal was the confidence in his wisdom and ability, and, above all, in the goodness and purity of his aims, that in a contest with him any one man, or squad of men, would be indignantly cloven down. By others popularity must be wooed before it is won ; to him it came spontaneously on every breeze from the sterile hills of New Hampshire and from the remotest savannahs of that land of promise which he had recently added to the Union. While Washington had been unable to command the vote of the Virginia delegation in either house of Congress, and could only secure the ratification of the British treaty, on which he had set his heart, by a bare majority, the senators from his own state voting against it, it was only necessary for Mr. Jefferson to express a wish in favor of a measure to ensure its success. To go to war with such a man was to extinguish all hope of successful ambition. On the other hand it may well be thought strange, that a man, who had aided in bringing an administration into power, had de-

fended all its acts, and with the warmest zeal those most
odious to its opponents, and had recently confessed his
conviction of the honesty and purity of the men at the
head of affairs, should suddenly turn about, and, disappro-
ving a system of temporary policy, which his friends had
been compelled, at an extraordinary period, to adopt, not
for its intrinsic worth, but as the lesser of two evils, should
not only draw the sword against them but fling away the
scabbard. His efforts in such a position were any thing
but refreshing. He was at once plunged into the midst of
the federal party. Politicians have long memories. Men,
who for the past seven years had been gritting their teeth
at him across the desks of the House of Representatives,
who believed that Randolph, though on their side to-day,
might, if he were consistent, on a change of policy, be on
the other to-morrow, and who knew better than he did the
terrible strength of the administration, thought themselves
sufficiently complaisant in adjusting their faces to a smile.
To add to his embarrassment, though a few personal friends
in and out of Congress upheld him, he saw in the popularity of the President, which was constantly increasing,
that all his aspirations, if he had any, must henceforth be
confined to the bosom in which they rose. Such was the
state of things at the close of this period.

Of the epoch extending from 1806 to the close of the
war in 1815, the representatives in the Convention were
more numerous. In its course Madison, who was to write
his celebrated letters to Erskine, which, like those of Mr.
Jefferson to Hammond, still exhibit the finest models of
diplomatic writing in our history, and was to put forth his
answer to Stephen, whose " War in Disguise" was the
text-book of the foreign and domestic foes of his administration, had become President, calling to the state department in due time his ancient coadjutor Monroe, with whom

he had adjusted, much to the annoyance of others, a very promising quarrel. Giles was the right arm of the dominant party in the Senate and had new duties to perform; for Randolph had not only abdicated the leadership in the House, but had become an enemy. Randolph, Garnett, McCoy, Bayly, Pleasants, Philip P. Barbour and Taliaferro, were at different times members of the House of Representatives. Randolph still continued in his solitary path, opposing the policy of commercial restrictions, and, what was singular enough, the war. He seemed to be alike unwilling that the administration should defend the country against the commercial despotism of France and England by legislative enactments and by the sword. He would not only allow our merchant ships to be seized, our sailors to be impressed, and our property to be confiscated by England, in violation of the laws of nations and of her own municipal law, but, though the ships of the enemy filled our waters and his feet were pressing our soil, he was unwilling that the administration should use either law or lead in our defence. His efforts, though frequent and long-continued, were of no avail, unless it be affirmed that the equivocal merit was his of transferring the honor of acquiring Florida from Thomas Jefferson to John Quincy Adams, whose pen at a later day was to win its fairest trophy in accomplishing a measure of such vital importance to the Southern States. Yet it was during this period that he spoke with the greatest preparation, and one of his speeches was not only republished in England with a laudatory preface by Stephen, the author of War in Disguise, but had the honor, then deemed no trifling one, of a review in the Edinburg; and it is to this period that the admirers of Randolph must look for the most vigorous productions of his mind. His speech on Gregg's resolution is one of his greatest efforts, and, if it has not the polish of his later speeches, it shows the body of his mind in bolder relief. But, if Mr. Randolph gained reputation abroad, he lost it throughout the Union and at home. The state of Georgia, which had hailed his talents with enthusiastic applause, became so indignant at his course, that she blotted his name from her statute book and from her map. And in 1813 he was no longer returned to the House.

Of the new members who appeared in the House of Representatives during this period none has made a more lasting impression on the country, and won greater distinction for himself, than PHILIP PENDLETON BARBOUR. He came in toward its close. He had defended the administration in the Assembly and before the people, and was about to embark on a new and dangerous sea. But we must trace him in the Convention. That body was fortunate in availing itself, on the retirement of Mr. Monroe, of the services of such a man at its most difficult crisis. He had filled the Speaker's chair in the House of Representatives, and brought to his new office the knowledge and the tact which the occasion demanded. If he had not the personal presence of his friend Clay, or of another eminent Virginian who afterwards filled the chair of the House of Representatives, he was, perhaps, superior to either in a knowledge of the logic and law of parliament. The most intricate skein of parliamentary difficulties seemed to unravel at his touch, and such was the confidence in his judgment and sense of honor, that his decisions, which were almost electric, were always satisfactory. As a speaker, his great aim seemed to be to apply mathematical reasoning to moral and political topics, and to give his speeches the terseness and pith of a judicial decision. Few productions could stand the test of his severe analysis; and it is said that Mr. Clay, as his published speeches show, would not take the floor on constitutional questions until Barbour had spoken. His voice was shrill and sharp; too angular for the public ear. His speech on the basis question is a fair sample of his mode of conducting an argument. He spoke with great fluency, and with much emphasis and gesticulation, and, intent on demonstrating the case in hand, thought the form of his argument needed not the aid of drapery. He was apt to apply his own standard of style and manner in estimating the eloquence of others, and when a person spoke in his presence of the eloquence of Daniel Webster, he admitted in all their extent the reasoning powers of that distinguished statesman, but not only denied his title to eloquence but the title of any man born east of the Hudson. Settling his creed in early life on the solid basis of demonstration, he continued to the end of his career the unfaltering advocate of all its great doctrines; and, although, unfortunately for his consistency, he was prevailed upon to withdraw his opposition to the bill incorporating the late bank of the United States, which was sure to pass without his vote, yet all the persuasions of Mr. Madison, whose representative he was, and of other friends, could not prevail upon him to follow the example of the party which had carried the country triumphantly through the war, and sustain that measure. He was about the middle height, remarkably thin, and rarely in robust health. He was plain in his dress, simple in his tastes, retiring in his habits. His early education was defective, and, although he had a general notion of what the Latin classics contained, there was that incompleteness in his knowledge which usually marks attainments in the languages made late in life, and he was more apt to make out the Latin from the sense than the sense from the Latin. Of course, he was altogether unversed in the critical niceties of that language; a defect which would have passed unobserved but for the frequent attempts which he made in the teeth of the rule of Horace to coin words of his own. Hence it might well happen that persons who observed his attempts in philology which he thought he understood but of which he was really ignorant, would be prone to draw very unfair conclusions respecting his knowledge on other subjects as well as of his general ability. A strict economist from principle, he could walk with the Guyon of Spencer untempted amid the glittering treasures of the cave of Mammon ; and when the state of Virginia remitted him what in those days was deemed a large fee for his services in the case of Cohens, he declined receiving it. It was on this occasion that he first came in contact with William Pinkney who was counsel for the appellants, and of whom, long after the grave had closed above that eminent lawyer, he ever spoke in terms of high admiration. He was a close student, and, amid the distractions of a long public career, never lost sight of the law. When a friend once called upon him during the winter of the Convention, he found him reading one of the volumes of Reports which had just appeared, and which, he said, afforded him a choice entertainment. He paid but little attention to literature, and in the lighter departments of letters he was so uninformed as never to have heard of Major Dugald Dalgetty of Drumthwacket, until Mr. Randolph introduced him to his acquaintance, and some time after, learning from a letter of a friend the history of the Major, he told it to his associates as a piece of news. Like Mansfield, he was more attached to law than to politics, and would have preferred the first seat on the bench to the first seat in the cabinet. In 1836, after a short term of service in the District Court, his aspirations were gratified with a seat on the bench of the Supreme Court. He had now attained the goal of his ambition, and all his faculties were called into full play. The federal constitution had been the study of his life, and the leading cases of the reports involving a conflict of the powers of the state and federal governments were well known to him ; but there were departments of the law, reared, during the third of a century then past, by a Stowell in the British Courts, and by Marshall and Story in our own, that were in a measure new to him ; for, living within the shadow of the Blue Ridge, those important topics of his profession which bore the fragrance of the sea had not been brought ordinarily before him. But with Barbour to see a defect was to mend it ;—to have an object in view was, as far as industry and sheer ability could go, to attain it. He was of all men whom I have known most devoted to an advancement in knowledge. He never stood still, nor halted by the wayside. He went from topic to topic. The acquisitions of one year became the solid foundations of those of the next. I have said that the law was his master passion. He loved those studies which are the handmaids of the law. Political economy and history were his delight. Not that history which Dr. Johnson defined to be the best, and which modern historians approve,—a history of morals or manners, but the political history of a country. Man in his political, not in his social, capacity was his study. He passed without interest over the description of a great battle, but looked closely to its results. Marathon, Morat, Waterloo, were soon read, but he never was tired of looking at the details of the Achaian or Amphyctionic league, of the Swiss confederation, of that condition of France when the feather of a Duke of Burgundy overshadowed the house of Orleans, or when the departments were amalgamated into a single system, and of the state of Europe when it was cut up by the sword of Napoleon and cut down by the goose-quill of Castlereagh. It was his misfortune never to have had access to a good library of the law ;—one that held its antiquities and the great landmarks in its history. Nothing would have afforded him more exquisite delight than to have been able, instead of resting on the authority of Coke, to trace for himself Magna Charta through all its confirmations back to Runnimede and from Runnimede forward to the time when an elector of Hanover sat upon a British throne. As his learning was ever in the field of facts, not of imagination, he was irresistible in conversational debate. The recollection of the conflict at a Wistar party in Philadelphia between Mathew Carey and himself is still a subject of mirth to those who saw the discomfiture of the champion of a different system from his own. In his new sphere on the federal bench an illimitable field stretched far and wide before him. With the gigantic mind of Marshall he had long been intimate—in the very body in which he then sat, in the debate on the judicial tenure, he had sensibly felt its force ; but it was in his daily associations with the accomplished Story that he learned to feel, perhaps for the first time, the undying grace which letters shed upon the law. His improvement during the four years he sat upon the bench was striking. In an elegant tribute to his memory Judge Story states, that "during his brief career in the Supreme Court, he widened and deepened the foundations of his judicial learning to an extraordinary extent; his reputation constantly advanced, and his judgments were listened to with increased respect and profound confidence. If he had lived many years with good health, he would not have failed to have won the highest distinction for all those qualities which give dignity and authority to the bench. It might be truly said of him that he was not only equal to all the functions of his high station but above them—*par negotiis et supra.* His country has lost by his death not only a bright ornament but a pure and spotless patriot.'

A beautiful tribute from one who was himself worthy of all praise, and who, like Barbour, is now only seen through that glorious light which exalted genius and virtue cast upon the grave. As it was, Virginia delighted to behold in Barbour the venerated name of her Pendleton invested with a new and appropriate illustration.

The fourth epoch in the organization of parties, extending from 1815, when the financial measures consequent upon the war with England which had just terminated, were adopted, to the period of the assembling of the Convention, embraced the history of some of the most eminent men in the body. Monroe soon succeeded Madison in the Presidency. Marshall was still on the bench. Giles, who was to yield to the thunderstorm, the first blasts of which he had defied, had not at the beginning of this period resigned his seat in the Senate. Tazewell was to begin his splendid career in the same body, in which his father had sat before him, both father and son succeeding, at a long interval, the same individual, the late John Taylor of Caroline. Pleasants, Randolph, and Tyler, during this period, also held seats in the Senate, Tazewell and Tyler at that time being the representatives of Virginia in that body. In the House of Representatives, Mercer, who in our own House of Delegates had attained distinction, and in the establishment of the Literary Fund had reared an imperishable memorial of his wisdom and benevolence, was to make his appearance. Alexander, Philip P. Barbour, John S. Barbour, McCoy, Pleasants, Powell, Randolph, Roane, Smith, and Tyler, were also at various times members of the House. A more brilliant delegation was rarely, if ever, contributed by a single state to the federal councils. Of the living I may not speak at length, and I regret that in this hurried sketch I am compelled to pass over so many of the dead. Randolph, who had resumed his seat in the House at the next Congress after his defeat, appeared henceforth in a more auspicious light. The policy which had separated him from his early friends for the past ten years was at an end. Now it was his good fortune to remain, as he said on another occasion, *rectus in curia*, and his ancient friends of the dominant party, who were to expunge some of their own principles from their creed, were to bend before him. A new scene in political affairs presented itself. The public debt was enhanced many millions. Taxes must be levied to pay the interest and to create a sinking fund for the ultimate redemption of the principal. Manufacturers, which grew up during the restrictive policy and the war, now appealed to the friends of those measures in their behalf. All the expedients of finance were soon found to be necessary, and a bill to incorporate a bank of the United States was brought in by those who had nobly sustained the honor of the country through the perilous period which had just closed, but who had hitherto contested the constitutionality of such a measure. Randolph, for the first time in the past ten years, stood in the broad sunlight of his ancient faith. Free from the responsibility of providing for the results of a policy which he had steadily opposed, he had no inducement to depart from his principles and embark in a new crusade. He thought that, if a bank was unconstitutional when Jefferson delivered his written opinion on the subject in the cabinet of Washington, and when Madison made his great speech against it in the House of Representatives and prepared a veto for Washington in the event of his deciding to return a bill incoporating such an institution to Congress, it was unconstitutional then. And if it was unconstitutional as late as 1811, when the old bank sought a renewal of its charter, and was denounced by the dominant party, it was unconstitutional then. And on the score of expediency,

if it were inexpedient when the federal government was
just stepping from its cradle under the guidance of Washington, when our foreign and domestic debts were un-
provided for—when the very price of liberty was unpaid,—
when our population, then small in numbers, had but recently exchanged the camp for the counting-house and the
sword for the plough;—it was not less so, at a time when
our country reached, not from Maine to Georgia, but from
the Passamoquoddy to the Gulf of Mexico,—when our
numbers had more than tripled;—when our commercial
marine had borne our flag in every sea, and brought to our
shores the treasures of every clime, and surpassed the
tonnage of every nation except England under the sun.
But he was to stand almost alone. Did Madison blush as
he signed that bill? Did Marshall, when from that serene
throne on which he had been sitting for sixteen years, and
who, in a few years, was to record for distant ages his
great decision in its favor, look over the ayes and noes on
the passage of the bill with a smile of triumph or a sneer?
Did Monroe, who had received on his person some of the
sturdiest blows of the opposite party when Washington was
its nominal head, and who was deemed a martyr in the republican cause—did Monroe, in the State Department or
at the Council board, shed a solitary tear over the departed
dogma? Did Randolph, on the passage of that bill, grieve
more for the constitution which he believed to be violated
in the house of its friends, than he rejoiced as he saw his
ancient friends, who had read him out of the republican
church, involved in the meshes of a policy from which his
intuitive sagacity foresaw that they could not extricate
themselves for a generation to come? There they are—
Madison, Marshall, Monroe, Randolph,—gathered for the
first time together under the same roof and in the same
hall—they can speak for themselves.

Of all the members of the Convention Mr. Randolph excited the greatest curiosity. Not a word that fell from his lips escaped the public ear, not a movement the public eye. When he rose to speak, the empty galleries began to fill, and when he ended, and the spell was dissolved, the throng passed away. It was on the 14th of November he made his first speech. Mr. Stanard had just concluded his speech, and the question on the amendment of Judge Green to the resolution of the Legislative committee basing the representation in the House of Delegates on white population exclusively was about to be taken, when he rose to address the chair. The word passed through the city in an instant that Randolph was speaking, and soon the house, the lobby, and the gallery, were crowded almost to suffocation. He was evidently ill at ease when he began his speech, but soon recovered himself when he saw the telling effect of every sentence that he uttered. He spoke nearly two hours, and throughout that time every eye was fixed upon him, and among the most attentive of his hearers were Mr. Madison and Mr. Monroe, who had not heard him before since his rupture with the administration of their predecessor in the Presidency. From that day he addressed the body with perfect self-possession, and although he did not at any subsequent time speak at length, he frequently mingled with marked ability in debate ; and it was easy to tell from the first sentence that fell from his lips when he was in fine tune and temper, and on such occasions the thrilling music of his speech fell upon the ear of that excited assembly like the voice of a bird singing in the pause of the storm. It is difficult to explain the influence which he exerted in that body. He inspired terror to a degree that even at this distance of time seems inexplicable. He was feared alike by East and West, by friend and foe. The arrows from his quiver, if not dipped in poison, were pointed and barbed, rarely missed the mark, and as seldom failed to make a rankling wound. He seemed to paralyse alike the mind and body of his victim. What made his attack more vexatious, every sarcasm took effect amid the plaudits of his audience. He called himself on one occasion a tomahawker and a scalper, and, true to the race from which he sprung, he never explained away or took back any thing; and, as he knew the private as well as the public history of every prominent member, it was impossible for his opponents to foresee from what quarter and on whom his attacks would fall. He also had political accounts of long standing to settle with sundry individuals, and none could tell when the day of reckoning would arrive. And when it did come, it was a stern and fearful one. What unnerved his opponents was a conviction of his invulnerability apparent or real; for, unconnected as he was by any social relation, and ready to fall back on a colossal fortune, he was not on equal terms with men who were struggling to acquire a competency, and whose hearts were bound by all the endearing ties of domestic love. Moreover, it was impossible to answer a sneer or a sarcasm with an argument. To attempt any thing of the kind was to raise a laugh at one's expense. Hence the strong and the weak in a contest with him were upon the same level.

In early youth the face of Mr. Randolph was beautiful, and its lineaments are in some degree preserved in his portrait by Stuart; but, as he advanced in life, it lost its freshness, and began to assume that aspect which the poet Moore described in his diary as a young-old face, and which is so faithfully pourtrayed by Harding. His voice, which was one of the great sources of his power, ranged from tenor to treble. It had no base notes. Its volume was full at times; but, though heard distinctly in the hall and the

galleries, it had doubtless lost much of the sweetness and
roundness of earlier years. Its sarcastic tones were on a
high key. He was, too, though he had the art to conceal
his art from common observers, a consummate actor. In
the philosophy of voice and gesture, and in the use of the
pause, he was as perfect an adept as ever trod the boards
of Covent Garden or Drury Lane. When he described
Chapman Johnson as stretching his arm to intercept and
clutch the sceptre as it was passing over Rockfish Gap,
or when he rallied him for speaking not "fifteen minutes as
he promised, but two hours, not by Shrewsbury clock, but
by as good a watch as can be made in the city of London,"
and, opening the case of his hunting watch, held it up to
the view of the chairman; or, when seeking to deride the
length of Johnson's speech, he said: "The gentleman said
yesterday, or the day before, or the day before that,"
Garrick or Kean would have crowned his acting with applause. No weight of character, no grade of intellect,
afforded a shield impenetrable by his shafts. Probably the
committee to which was referred near its close all the resolutions of the Convention with a view of having them
drawn in the form of a constitution, was the most venerable in years, in genius, in all the accomplishments of the
human mind, and in length and value of public service,
that ever sat on this side of the Atlantic. Madison, Marshall, Tazewell, Doddridge, Watkins Leigh, Johnson, and
Cooke were the seven members who composed it. Yet
Mr. Randolph, almost without an effort, raised a laugh at
their expense. It appears, if I am not mistaken, that some
qualification of the right of suffrage, which was embraced
in the resolutions, was not to be found in the reported
draft, and to this omission Mr. Randolph called the attention of the house. Mr. Leigh observed that, if Mr. Randolph's views were carried out, it would virtually leave

the entire regulation of the right of suffrage to the General Assembly. Randolph replied with all his peculiar emphasis and gesture: " Sir, I would as soon trust the house of burgesses of the commonwealth of Virginia as the committee of *seven*." I followed his finger, and amid the roar of laughter which burst forth, I saw Mr. Madison and Mr. Leigh suddenly and unconsciously bow their heads. He idolised Shakspear, and cherished a taste for the drama; and in this department of literature as well as in that of the older English classics from Elizabeth to Anne, and indeed, in all that was embraced by the curiosity and taste of a scholar, his library was rich. He spoke and wrote the English language in all its purity and elegance, and his opponents had at least the gratification of knowing that they were abused in good English. Indeed Madison could not vie with him in a full and ready control over the vocabulary or the harmony of the English tongue. His later speeches exemplify this remark in a more striking manner than his earlier ones. In his speech on Retrenchment delivered in the House of Representatives in 1828, one meets with sentences of great beauty, and it may be observed, that toward the close of that speech is one of the few pathetic touches to be found in his productions. Yet it may well be doubted whether his speeches will hold a high place in after times. His sayings will be quoted in the South, and some of his speeches will undoubtedly be read; but they will hardly emerge beyond Mason and Dixon's line, and never reach even within that limit the dignity of models. What Sir James McIntosh observed to an American respecting one of his speeches will probably convey, when oral tradition grows faint, the impression which they make on impartial minds,—that there was a striving after effect—a disposition to say smart or hard things beyond the ability. On the score of argument they were beneath criticism. It is but just, however, to say that Mr. Randolph protested against the authenticity of most of the speeches attributed to him. Those in the published debates of the Convention are undoubtedly authentic, and must have received his revisal. But of his eloquence thus much may fairly be said, that it fulfilled its office in its day and generation ; for it is unquestionably his praise that above all his contemporaries he was successful in fixing the attention of his audience of every class and degree throughout his longest speeches. The late Timothy Pitkin, a competent judge, who had known Randolph many years in Congress, observed, at a time when it was fashionable to compare Tristram Burgess with him, that you may as well compare the broadsword of a mosstrooper with the scymitar of Saladin. When it is remembered that Mr. Randolph, at all times infirm, was sometimes during the winter of the Convention in his own opinion at the point of death, it is a fact of great import, that at no other period of his career did he speak with more judgment and acuteness, nor on any other occasion did he so entirely gain the regards of the people of Eastern Virginia, or his genius excite greater admiration than by his exhibition in that body.

As we began this division of our subject with the name of Madison, we may not unfitly close it with a name which has been intimately associated with his for half a century, and which, though it has been prominently put forth already, calls for, at least so far as the Convention is concerned, a few passing remarks. The name of JAMES MONROE has yet to receive the exalted appreciation which it deserves, and which posterity will surely award. He lived so near our own time ;—his administration gave birth to so many important questions about which parties have formed and rallied, that it is only from the pen of the historian, who from the vantage ground of the distant future shall look back upon the past, that his character will receive a full and candid illustration. Allusion has been made to his service in the field during the Revolution, to his course in the Virginia federal convention, his mission to France, his election to the Senate of the United States, his mission to Great Britain, his nomination to the war and to the state department, and his elevation to the Presidency as the successor of the illustrious man whom he followed step by step throughout a long and glorious life. If to these appointments be added his election to the House of Delegates, especially in 1810, when he made a speech remarkable rather by the illustrations drawn from the history of the French Republic which he had personally observed, and the sound practical views with which it abounded, than by rhetorical skill, and his election to the office of Governor of this Commonwealth, the list of the offices held by him will be nearly complete. Of all the men who had filled the office of President of the United States to the period of his election to that high station, with the exception of Washington, his person was the most generally known by the people. He had mingled so freely with his fellow-men abroad and at home;—he had so frequently come in personal contact with the generation in which he lived, that hundreds of people who had never seen a more important personage than a captain in the army or navy, a member of Congress, or at most the head of a department, had not only seen him but shaken hands with him, and heard from his honest lips words of kindness and regard. He was borne into the presidential chair of the Union without a contest. His election and re-election seemed a matter of course. Strangely as it may sound in our ears, there was a prestige of military glory about him, which bound him to the hearts of the people. He was the first incumbent of the chair since Washington filled it, who had seen the flash of a hostile gun, and had drawn his sword in defence of his country. As has been said, the time is not come, when an impartial history of his administration can be written; but we may be allowed to say that the most brilliant and honprable career that was ever presented to an American president was then before him. Washington, Adams, Jefferson, and Madison, were beset with difficulties foreign and domestic, which consumed their entire terms of office. When Monroe came into power, the perplexities in our foreign affairs, which in one shape or other from the peace of Paris to near the close of Madison's term had worried every administration, and which, if they did not create, kept alive the party organizations of the day, were at an end. If we except a solitary question which had been settled for a term of years, a *carte blanche* of our foreign and domestic policy was within the grasp of his hand. In the selection of his cabinet, so far as the talents and the patriotism of its members were concerned, he was most fortunate. If we exclude the first administration of Washington, the country had not seen so able a cabinet. But, with the single remark that, whatever may be the opinions entertained of its policy, there was but one opinion of the honesty and unblemished purity of its head, we drop a veil over this portion of his history.

When Mr. Madison nominated Mr. Monroe for the chair of the Convention, he was aware of his physical inability to perform any laborious service; but he might have remembered that Pendleton, who presided in the Virginia federal convention, was in appearance more of an invalid than Monroe, and had performed the duties of the office with the recorded approbation of the body. But the nature of the two bodies was wholly dissimilar. In the federal convention, the main object of which was to consider

a constitution ready made, and which must be accepted or
rejected as a whole, the discussions were conducted in the
committee of the whole altogether, and the president was
only called upon to occupy the chair for a few moments
at the beginning and at the close of the daily session.   Of
the twenty seven days during which the convention held
its sittings, Pendleton probably did not preside three entire
days.   The ayes and noes were called but three times during the session.   The Convention of 1829-30 presented a
very different scene.   Here was no constitution ready
made and to be ratified or rejected as a whole, but a constitution was to be made under circumstances of extraordinary delicacy.   There was hardly a prominent member
who had not a plan of his own on paper or in his brain,
or, if his scheme did not embrace an entire system, it fas-
tened on one of the great departments.   Others came
charged with a reformation of the County Courts, the abo-
lition of the Council, and the regulation of the right of
suffrage.   The members on the most important question of
the day had made up their minds, and one great division
of the state was arrayed against the other.   To preside in
such a body required not only a critical knowledge of the
law of parliaments, and the utmost readiness in its application, but a capacity of physical endurance which is not
often possessed by men who have passed the prime of life.
It is true that much was done in committee of the whole ;
but the final battle on every question must be fought in
the house.   For such a station, which required such a rare
ability of mind and body, it is not uncourteous to say that
Mr. Monroe, who was never much conversant with public
assemblies, and was more infirm than either Madison or
Marshall, was wholly unfit.   Fortunately, before the day
of severe trial came, he withdrew from the house, and left
the toil and the honor of his responsible position to another.

Yet, while he remained a member, he engaged more than once in discussion ; and, though, at that period of intense excitement, his speech on the basis was listened to more as a means of knowing on which side of a question which was ultimately decided in a house of ninety six members by two votes his vote would be cast, rather than from any regard of its matter or its manner of delivery, he spoke more readily, and with greater self-possession, than might have been anticipated from one so advanced in life and so long retired from popular bodies. His animated description of the murder of a member in the midst of the French National Convention by a mob which marched among the members with the severed head of their victim stuck upon a pole ; a murder which was perpetated in his presence while he was the minister near the Republic, and which, though he had described it in his speech in the House of Delegates twenty years before, was heard by most of the members for the first time, made a strong impression. The resignation of the chair and of his seat was received with the deepest respect, and there was a shade of sorrow on every face when it was officially stated that his venerable form would be seen in that hall no more, and that so great and so good a name would no longer adorn the records of the house.

I have thus far dwelt on that aspect of the Convention which presented the greatest attraction to persons from abroad ; it is now my purpose to regard it more in the light in which it appeared among ourselves. The members who had served in the federal councils deserved all the consideration which they enjoyed ; but those who had not then appeared beyond our limits possessed abilities of the highest order, and had won a distinguished reputation at home. And it was soon seen that upon them mainly devolved the most important labors of the body. Doddridge,

Upshur, Morris, Baldwin, Scott, Cooke, Joynes, Broadnax, Summers, Fitzhugh, Johnson, Leigh, and others, busily engaged in the pursuits of private life, had not passed beyond the limits of Virginia, but had long been engaged in her service, and excited the greatest interest among the people. There was also a brilliant coterie of a younger date, who had already been prominent in the Assembly, and were destined to rise to still greater distinction abroad; and let me say to you, sir, that nothing so much impresses upon my mind the rapidity with which we are passing away, as the reflection that nearly three score years have rolled over the heads of Mason of Southampton, Mason of Frederick, Goode, Morgan, Gordon, Loyall, Logan, Moore, Thompson, and others of that gallant groupe ; and I am sure you will join with me in paying the passing tribute of a tear to the memory of one—not the least brilliant of them all—the lamented Dromgoole. But to our task.

It will be remembered that the first great speech on the basis question was pronounced by Judge ABEL PARKER UPSHUR of Northampton. He had spent his youth at Princeton, and early devoted himself to the study of the law. He entered the House of Delegates in 1819, and was a member at intervals until his elevation to the bench of the General Court, of which he was then a member. He was in the full vigor of manhood, having just attained his fortieth year. He was called unexpectedly to the floor, but he more than fulfilled the public expectation. His commanding person, his graceful and animated action, the unequalled strength and beauty of his argument, the accidental yet fortunate position he occupied on the floor, which enabled him to see and be seen by the hundreds who thronged that hall, produced a fascinating effect. Persons from abroad, who had come to listen to the eloquence of the eminent

E.T.S.U. AT TEXARKANA LIBRARY

men whose names had become the household words of the
country, heard his speech during the two days of its delivery with astonishment mingled with delight. The East
could not have opened the campaign under more favorable
auspices. Nor was the effect of the speech on the body
itself less remarkable. It was as conclusive on the branch
of the subject which it discussed as ever speech could be,
and hermetically sealed a fountain which had been gushing copiously for years. Few speakers possessed in the
same degree with him the faculty of subtle disquisition,
and in the House of Delegates he had frequently displayed
great skill in debate. There are those now present, perhaps, who remember his contest in that body with the late
Gen. Blackburn, who, himself the hero of a hundred fights,
confessed his power. Nor was his eloquence exhibited in
public discussion only. He was as great with his pen as
with his tongue. His address before the Historical Society, written on a topic of vital interest to the South, has
not yet received full credit for the cogency of its logic and
the beauty of its style. He was a native of the Eastern
Shore ;—a slip of country, which, however rich in its soil,
is still richer in the genius and patriotism of its sons, and
which then contributed an able delegation to the body. It
is mournful to think that such a man, when he was called
to a sphere commensurate with his fine abilities, was so
suddenly taken away.

With all who are conversant with the legislative history
of the state the name of PHILIP DODDRIDGE has long been
familiar. Perhaps, to him more than to any other man
living, disconnected from the public press, the Convention
then sitting owed its existence. As early as 1816, with
Smythe and Mercer, he had fought the battle in the House
of Delegates with success, but his favorite measure was
defeated in the Senate. Then, and not till then, did he

approve the passage of the bill re-arranging the Senatorial
districts on the basis of white population. Although he
never entirely forgave the East because the districts were
re-arranged on the census of 1810, and for the loss of a
fraction of population which he thought was due to the
West, he was candid and generous in his appreciation of
the talents displayed by his opponents on that occasion, and
often in private, and more than once in debate, spoke of
the argument of Tazewell in reply to Gen. Smythe on the
convention-bill of that session as by far the ablest he had
ever heard in a deliberative assembly. A member of the
House of Delegates at intervals through a long tract of
time, he was in that body during the session of 1828-9,
when the bill calling the existing convention became a law,
and sustained it with a masterly speech. It may not be
unjust to the living or the dead to affirm that of all the
distinguished representatives from beyond the Ridge, he
held the first place in the estimation of the West. There
his early history was known ; there his fine talents brought
forth their first fruits ; and there was the theatre in which
his greatest forensic efforts were made. There was something, too, in the fortunes of a friendless youth, with no aid
but from his own untiring spirit, winning his way to the
highest distinction yet retaining to the last the simple
manners of early years, which appeals to the best feelings
of the human heart every where. The people of the West
knew and loved the man, but they had known and loved
the boy. The interview of the young Doddridge, chubby,
sunburnt, ungainly, and in his boatman's garb, with the
haughty governor of the Spanish territory on the Mississippi—neither understanding the native language of the
other, but conversing in bastard Latin which the youth had
picked up while his fellows were pinking squirrels out of
the tree-tops of the yet unbroken forests of the West,

would form a suggestive picture, which, I hope, the brush of some Western son of genius will commit to canvas for the admiration of future times. Well and worthily did he requite the affection of the West. Not only in his great speech on the basis question, when the hope of triumph was bright before him, but afterward, when his plans were thwarted, did he strive to secure the great object of his mission. As a speaker, he had many great qualities— readiness, fluency, and an unlimited command of all the logic, and, what was of great importance in that body, of all the statistics of his case. Irascible even, and prompt to take offence where offence was intended, he was distinguished for great courtesy in debate;—a trait so distinctly marked as to call forth the pointed acknowledgment of Randolph. Whether he prepared himself expressly for the occasion I cannot say—for the whole subject had been the study of years—but in the great debate on the basis, and in the innumerable ones which would suddenly spring up, he was a gushing fountain of facts and figures. He had none of the ordinary graces of a speaker about him. His voice seemed to come from his throat and had no freedom of play. He was low and broad in stature; his features were heavy, though to a close observer they might bespeak a great mind in repose; and in his dress he was a very sloven. Indeed his form and dress, even his position in the Convention as well as the powers of his great mind, are foreshadowed by Horace in his third satire as faithfully as if the Tiber and the Yohogany were sister streams:

> Iracundior est paulo; minus aptus acutis
> Naribus horum hominum; videri possit, eo quod,
> Rusticius tonso toga defluit, et male laxus
> In pede calceus hæret. At est bonus, ut melior vir
> Non alius quisquam; at tibi amicus; at ingenium ingens
> Inculto latet hoc sub corpore;

I have spoken of the readiness of Doddridge in debate. He was occasionally very happy in retort. When he was replying in the legislative committee, which held its sessions in the Senate chamber of that day, to an argument which Tazewell had just delivered, he remarked, alluding to the Convention bill of 1816, that he had heard that argument before. Tazewell observed audibly: *Ergo* it is unsound. Doddridge instantly retorted: *Ergo* it has been *answered* before. Though a resident of that region which has not inaptly been termed the pan handle of the state, and in his daily offices mingling more with the people of other states than with our own, he was as true a Virginian as ever trod our soil, and was among the last of our eminent statesmen who spoke with something of the acerbity of personal feeling of the craft with which the Pennsylvania commissioners, at the head of whom was the celebrated Rittenhouse, are reputed to have beguiled our own out of thousands of acres of our most fertile territory. On his return home he was elected to Congress, and, while engaged in reducing to a code the local laws of the District of Columbia,—an office for which he was peculiarly fitted, he was, like his colleagues Upshur and Barbour, suddenly cut off.

Another of those remarkable men who had not appeared in the federal councils, whose mind was formed to grapple with the most complicated topics in law and politics, and who took a prominent part in the proceedings of the Convention, was ROBERT STANARD. It was the singular honor of Richmond that the names of four such men as Marshall, Leigh, Johnson, and Stanard, were enrolled among its residents. But Stanard held his seat as the representative of another district. The ground he stood upon in the Convention was an elevated one. His appointment came from a district in which he had spent his early life, and which he had represented in the Assembly, but from which he had been separated for years. When Mr. Stanard rose to deliver his speech on the basis, Mr. Johnson had just concluded his great speech on that subject, which may well be supposed to have made a deep impression on his audience. Still the body was jaded and fagged, and the Western members, who anticipated a triumph, were anxious for the question. On the side of the East, which might gain but could not lose by delay, although the members were worn in some degree by the protracted discussion,—for it was as late as the fourteenth of November when Mr. Stanard began his speech, there was a strong desire not only that the speech of Johnson should be examined, but that certain epithets, such as aristocrat and the like, should be repelled, and the misrepresentations of some of the arguments of Judge Upshur on the principles of government should be corrected. What rendered such a coerrction necessary, was the fact that the East not only received no support from the press of Richmond, but found in its editors the most influential opponents of its favorite basis. And this leads me to say that there were sitting at the clerk's table, busily engaged in taking notes of the proceedings, two men, not members of the body, filling no civil office, who then wielded a greater influence over the people than any other two men in the State, and had long favored, though with very different ulterior views, a change in the fundamental law. The elder of these for a quarter of a century had edited a journal, which was the leading organ of the dominant party in the State, with a zeal and ability hitherto unknown in our annals, and with corresponding success. He had taught the people to think his own thoughts, to speak his own words, to weep when he wept, to wreathe their faces with his smiles, and, over and above all, to vote as he voted. A sovereignty so complete over the public mind was not likely to pass uncontested. Boys, who had just laid aside their satchels; statesmen who had lost office or sought it under a new system; writers of every degree, dipping their pens in ink not unmixed with gall, sought to impair it, and sought in vain. Popularity, running through a long lapse of years, and questioned at every step of its progress, is rarely an accident; and it is certain there was an abiding conviction that such influence was wielded by its possessor in a good cause, and that he was as honest as he was able. In person he was tall and lean; his profile so distinctly marked as not, if once seen, to be easily forgotten; quick in all his movements, and in his gait he leaned slightly forward. Nor did he spurn the duties of the toilet. In this respect at least he had no mark of the professional devil about him. In the relations of life he was eminently courteous and social, and withal was the most laborious man of his age. The editor of a daily commercial paper and a semi-weekly political one must be a busy man. For many years he drew largely on the small hours of the morning. I have spoken of his tact as a party manager. He never lost his temper. He may have acted unwisely, but never rashly or foolishly. If he was sometimes seen to trip or fall, it was only to rise again, like Antæus, with redoubled strength. All parties have their family troubles. It would happen at times that a politician, who was persuaded by his friends that he did not enjoy that consideration in the party to which he was entitled, would run restive; and it was amusing to see the skill with which our editor would reeve a cord through his nose and lead him cosily about. But it was mainly when a politician abjured his allegiance and joined the opposite party, that his full force was felt. The abuse of his quondam Palinurus was the burden of the rebel's song, and if the abuse of enemies constituted moral wealth in the eyes of friends, he would have been the richest man in the country. Nor did this abuse affect his equanimity ; for in his busy life it became a matter of course, and he may be said never to have been at peace but in a state of war— never out of trouble but when in it. But, as THOMAS RITCHIE still lives, it is beyond our present purpose to say farther than that all the influence of such a character was thrown on the convention question into the scale of the West.

The other person then sitting near him was much younger in years, small in stature, careless in his apparel, his face bearing a weight of premature care—a prophetic face, which was redeemed by a brilliant eye. His intellectual endowments were of a high order. In wit, sarcasm, scorn— in a ready command of the choicest words and phrases— in a knowledge of men and things passing before him, and in those qualifications which make up a dashing editorial, he had no superior—hardly an equal. His writings made a new era in our newspaper literature. Some of his finer touches were beyond the reach of FONBLANQUE. He made enemies, as all men, who in exciting times bring positive qualities to bear on exciting topics, are prone to make : yet there were few of his political opponents who did not occasionally relish his raillery even when it played upon their own party. He sometimes fell into amusing mistakes : for he had read history rather by dwelling on favorite eras, within the range of which he delighted to linger, than at large, and he was apt, in the hurry of the moment, to gather his knowledge at second hand ; and the lightnings of his genius often scorched too severely the objects on which they fell. Nor did he possess—perhaps he scorned it—that exquisite tact which is required in a public leader in a country like ours, and which was the prominent characteristic of his great opponent ; for, with the single exception of the convention question, THOMAS RITCHIE and JOHN HAMPDEN PLEASANTS held no political topic in unison; but on that common ground they plied their constant task. Hence, as the East had no representative through the press, nothing could have been more opportune than the speech of Mr. Stanard. He opened magnificently on the " war of epithets," as he termed it, and analysed the arguments of Johnson with wonderful skill, carrying out his concessions to results which were as unexpected to Johnson as to his audience at large. When he had brushed away all the false guises which he thought had concealed the true question at issue, he proceeded to discuss it, dwelling incidentally on the arguments of the members who had preceded him in debate, and subjecting them to the test of the severest logic. He recalled to the attention of the house an argument of Mr. Leigh on the results likely to flow from a rejection of the federal basis by a Southern State, showed that it had been evaded, or not met at all, and urged it with such force as to make a deep impression on the body. From his habits of thorough analysis and his high mathematical attainments he was well qualified to examine the doctrine which had been urged in debate of the applicability of the exact sciences to politics, and he performed the office with great ability. He spoke from the conclusion of Mr. Johnson's speech to the adjournment, and for the larger part of the next day, and was listened to with untiring interest by members on both sides of the house; for not among the least interesting parts of his address were the interlocutory discussions that arose on the part of those whose arguments were subjected to his searching examination. His speech is reported with considerable fullness, and it is to this speech that a majority of readers, not familiar with the law reports, must look in forming their opinions of his ability as a public speaker and the qualities of his intellect. With the proper qualifications with which one should read such a speech, taken down by a stenographer, and corrected, if at all, by the speaker when the glow of the moment is gone, it will be found to sustain the burden of a large and vigorous reputation. He dallied not in flowery meads or by the banks of flowing streams; he left Shakspear and Milton—the drama and the epic—to the other members of the committee to use or abuse as they pleased ; but every word that he uttered—every sentence that fell from his lips—was a step in the progress of his argument,—was a link in that chain with which he bound his opponents. Epithets applied to persons had no place in his vocabulary; yet his speech was as personal as it well could be ; and the different explanations that were elicited during its delivery were as painful and more vexatious to the parties concerned, than if he had written the most opprobrious names on their foreheads. He was especially successful in annoying his opponents by collating their respective arguments and comparing them with each other—a tender office, which in his hands was apt to breed trouble in political families. His speech and that of Upshur, though differing as widely as possible from each other, may be regarded among the finest models of parliamentary discussion to which the Convention gave birth. The speech of Joynes, incomparable in its way, was mainly limited to the financial view of his subject, and was not designed to embrace a full examination of the multiform principles which lie at the foundation of the social compact. With all our state affairs Stanard was intimately acquainted, having served his apprenticeship in the House of Delegates of which he had been the presiding officer, and it is worthy of remark that the discussions of the Convention were mainly conducted by men who had spent a term of service in that school ; and, perhaps, it may be said, that, if to any one source more than another the excellence of our public speakers may be attributed, it will be found in their early and habitual service in the General Assembly. If Mr. Stanard were able in debate, there were others who possessed in a far higher degree the perfections of an orator. He had a hesitancy in his speech, or the defect may have arisen from the habit of recalling his sentences in order to put them in another form, and his diction, though correct and at times caustic, did not abound in the graces which rarely pertain to those who refuse to pay their court at the shrine of the Muses. He was a strenu- ous advocate of the independence of the judiciary, and not approving of the provisions of the new constitution on the tenure of the judicial office, voted against its final adoption. He again entered the House of Delegates, and made a speech in opposition to the Expunging Resolutions, which was one of the most elaborate, most subtle, and most eloquent speeches ever pronounced within its walls. He was afterwards elected to the Court of Appeals, and at the time of his death held that station which he emi- nently adorned.

It would be amiss even in this hurried sketch of the emi- nent members of the Convention who had not appeared in the federal councils, to omit the name of Gen. ROBERT BAR- RAUD TAYLOR of Norfolk. He was educated at William and Mary, where he held a prominent position among the young men who then attended that institution. Rarely does it happen that a greater number of distinguished pupils were ever present at a single seminary at the same time than were then gathered in those classic halls. There was JOHN THOMPSON, the author of the Letters of Curtius addressed to Gen. Marshall,—one who I have heard his surviving class- mate declare was the most extraordinary young man he ever knew, and over whose early death Virginia well might mourn; JAMES BARBOUR, whose honorable career in our public councils as a member of the House of Delegates and of the Senate of the United States, Governor, Secretary at War, and Minister to the Court of St. James, is a part of our history; WILLIAM HENRY CABELL, who, having received the highest civil and judicial honors of his native State, and displaying in the society of the metropolis in which he moved for half a century an urbanity and grace peculiarly his own, died recently at an advanced age; JOHN RANDOLPH, who, brilliant as he was, was in the midst of his equals; and LITTLETON WALLER TAZEWELL, who then displayed those qualities which were to add new glory to a name already distinguished in our annals, and who, on the banks of the Elizabeth, in the midst of a lovely family, and in full possession of his great faculties, still survives. Strictly speaking, they were not classmates. Randolph and Tazewell studied Cordery together, and were classmates at the grammar school in Williamsburg for several years, but were not in college at the same time, Randolph having gone abroad and not returning to William and Mary until Tazewell had taken his degree. Thompson and Tazewell were classmates, but when Tazewell was in the senior class, Barbour, Cabell, and Taylor were in the junior, which Randolph did not join until it became senior.

The *physique* of these young men was as remarkable as their *morale*. Barbour, Cabell, and Tazewell were six feet high and upward; Taylor did not quite reach that standard of height, but was one of the most imposing and elegant men of the age. Thompson was about the height of Taylor, his features peculiar and far from handsome, with a grey lustrous eye. Randolph in early youth surpassed them all in beauty. A friend, who saw him with his mother in New York in 1786, spoke of him as a beautiful and

fascinating boy, and I have heard one of his schoolfellows
describe him as the most lovely youth he ever beheld, his
face exquisitely formed, his complexion brilliant, and his
eyes blacker, if possible, than in manhood. These were
the associates of Taylor in his college years, and with them
he pursued the study of the law. In the politics of early
life Gen. Taylor differed from his colleagues, and, while
they sustained the doctrines of the republican party, he
embraced those of the opposite school. All these young
men except Thompson almost immediately entered public
life. Cabell became a member of the House of Delegates
as early as 1795, where he remained, with an interruption
of three years, until 1805, when he was elected Governor,
and, on the expiration of his term, a judge of the General
Court, and afterward a judge of the Court of Appeals,
crowning his public life with the highest judicial honor
which Virginia could bestow. Barbour, Cabell, and Tazewell were members of the House of Delegates in 1798-99,
and supported John Taylor's resolutions; and in 1799—
1800, Barbour, Tazewell, and Taylor were members of that
body, the two first sustaining the report of Mr. Madison,
and the last opposing it. In 1799 Randolph took his seat
in the House of Representatives, in which body and in the
Senate, he spent nearly the whole period of his life. At
a later date there was a change in the political relations of
these young politicians. In 1806 Thompson was no more;
but from that time until 1816, Randolph in the House of
Representatives, and Taylor and Tazewell in private life,
opposed the administrations of Jefferson and Madison,
while Barbour and Cabell, both of whom filled the office of
Governor during this interval, sustained them. It was in
1809 that Gen. Taylor became a candidate for Congress in
the Norfolk district in opposition to Col. Newton the democratic nominee, and was defeated. Still, such was the

rank which Taylor held in his profession, having been engaged for nearly the third of a century on one side or other
of every important case in the Norfolk circuit, and so great
was his zeal in its pursuit, he had no time for studies not
bearing directly upon the business of life. Hence politics,
as a science, may be said hardly to have engaged his attention; and so slightly acquainted was he with the state
of parties and opinions in the commonwealth, that in a
speech before the people during the canvass, he proposed
as his favorite basis of representation the striking of one
member from each county,—a result highly acceptable to
his constituents, as it left the balance of power just as it
was,—and defended this scheme at length on the ground
of economy and expediency. It was not until the meeting of the body that the white basis was presented to his
view, when he embraced it with that zeal which marked
his character; and instantly arriving at the conclusion that
no other basis was consistent with a republican system,
and knowing that nineteen-twentieths of his constituents
were opposed to his views, he resigned his seat. His letter of resignation is fitly inscribed on the journal of the
Convention, and, elegant in point of composition, will reflect on future times the chivalry of his character and his
unspotted purity of purpose. When the Loudoun delegation elected him the successor of Mr. Monroe, he sent in
a graceful but prompt declination.

It has been stated that Gen. Taylor was opposed to the
policy of Mr. Madison; yet, when war was declared, unlike
his friend Randolph who refused to vote appropriations for
the public defence in flagrant war, he was among the first to
rally around the standard of his country. He was appointed
the commanding general of the forces at Norfolk, and, although no opportunity occurred of meeting the enemy, it
was well known that, in the event of an engagement, he

would have achieved all that undaunted valor could have won. On his retirement from service, Mr. Madison tendered him the appointment of a general officer in the regular army, but he declined the honor. With the exception of a seat in the House of Delegates in 1826–7, when he opposed with all his ability the Tariff resolutions of Mr. Giles, he held no civil office from the commencement of the century to the year 1830, when he was appointed judge of the Norfolk district under the new constitution—an office which he held but three years when his country was called upon to lament the death of one of the most devoted patriots and most accomplished men.

It was on the conclusion of Judge Barbour's speech that Gen. BRISCOE G. BALDWIN rose to address the house. He had long been a favorite son of the West. Some years previously he had been a member of the House of Delegates, and, associated with Sheffey, the Roger Sherman of the West, had exerted himself to effect the removal of the seat of government from Richmond to Staunton. In the discussions on that question he sustained himself with marked ability, and, if he did not succeed in his object, gained an increase of reputation. He was one of the finest looking men in the Convention, was six feet in height, and of commanding proportions; and he was most cordial in his address. The leading trait of his speech on the basis was its generous humanity. This is no common praise. At a time of high excitement such as then prevailed, it required no small degree of moral courage to talk of peace. He scorned a war among brethren, and made an eloquent appeal to the body in favor of extinguishing the passions of the moment at the altar of one common country. His manly form is fresh before me as he spoke that day. It may be said, that his speech, apart from the chivalric spirit which it breathed and inspired, though able, was not regarded by his friends as a fair exponent of his powers, nor did it quite come up to the full expectation of the country. He was elected to fill a vacancy in the Court of Appeals established by the constitution which he aided in framing, and remained on the bench till his court was superseded by the present constitution. And, on the eve of the recent election of the judges of the Court of Appeals by the people, when his name was again brought forth under the most favorable auspices, quite unexpectedly to all, he suddenly deceased.

If I omitted a more formal notice of ALFRED HARRISON POWELL in another place, it was because he more properly belonged here; as he spoke at length on the basis question, and succeeded Gen. Baldwin on the floor. He had established a reputation in the House of Representatives, and was known in the commonwealth not only as a politician, but as a gentleman of pure character and of a high sense of honor. Although he belonged to the East, he ranged under the banners of the West; and, however strong, as the West undoubtedly was, in the number and prowess of her champions, there were many who regarded Powell as likely to render service in the common cause as great as any which would be rendered by his colleagues who stood more prominently than he did before the people. He had been a member of the House of Delegates as well as of the House of Representatives, and was, perhaps, the most thoroughly skilled of his political associates in the practice of deliberative bodies. A knowledge of parliamentary tactics is at all times an element of power, and, as in the Convention skill was arrayed against numbers, was of the first moment to the interests of the West. He had a good person; his address was at once frank and refined; and it is probable that, if the honor of the presiding office of the body had been awarded by the West to any of her advocates on the score of individual fitness, Powell would have borne away the palm. Nor was the East insensible to his merit. He was more frequently called to the chair in committee than any other member; and his speech on the basis was looked for and listened to with corresponding interest. It was altogether a speech worthy of his reputation, and will show the caste of his mind as well as his style of debate; but, as he was indisposed when he spoke, it was not as effective in its delivery as it would otherwise have been; and a higher impression of his powers was received from his subsequent efforts. Few men appeared to have a stronger hold on life than his; but he survived the adjournment a few years only.

It was early in the debate on the basis that RICHARD MORRIS of Hanover made his speech. Not above the middle size, though not much beyond the prime of manhood nearly bald, with a face, if not handsome, animated and expressive, he advanced to the contest like a preux chevalier, who, having thrown aside for the moment his breastplate, and his sword, and his plumed helm, had descended to the arena of the council to advise those measures which he was ready to execute in the field. He had been trained in the House of Delegates, and was at home upon all State topics; and displayed at once that self-possession and vivacity in debate, which several speakers, his equals in intellect, failed to evince. His reputation as an orator and a debater may safely rest on the speech which he made in favor of the mixed basis. In his political sentiments he leaned in early life to the federal party, and was usually connected with that small but distinguished clique known as the tertium quids; and, as from his near residence to Richmond his influence was sensibly felt here, he may be classed with those politicians who succeeded in neutralizing the influence of Mr. Jefferson in the metropolis of his

native State. It was on the conclusion of his able and eloquent speech on the basis that Randolph made the play-
ful remark which moved the mirth of the West as well as
the East : " I see that the wise men still come from the
East." He did not engage in any subsequent discussion
that I now remember, and in less than three years after the
adjournment of the body of which he was one of the ablest
and most distinguished members, at an age hardly exceeding fifty-five, he died at his seat in Hanover.

The member who followed Morris in the debate on the
basis and whose election to a seat in that body was a topic
of remark at the time, from his unique position requires,
though still living, a short notice. In Virginia, before
and since the Revolution, a prejudice has existed in
the public mind on the subject of an union of religious
and political functions in the same person. In England
the clerical character is indelible, and in this State no cler-
gyman had appeared either in the State or Federal convention ; and he was directly excluded from the General
Assembly. It is true that Witherspoon was one of the
most efficient members of the Continental Congress, and
exerted a wholesome influence in settling in the articles of
Confederation—the identical basis for which the East was
then contending; and in our own State president Smith
of Hampden Sidney, in the discussions of the day on the
expediency of adopting the Federal constitution, had opposed Patrick Henry, who, in answer to Smith's pointed
enquiry why, instead of abusing the constitution, he had
not repaired to Philadelphia and aided the Convention with
his advice when it might have been of some avail, replied
with a significant look and gesture : " Sir, *I smelt a rat.*"
And not long before the meeting of the convention, Edward Everett, who had filled the churches of Boston with
crowds anxious to catch every syllable from his eloquent

lips, had thrown aside the gown, and had recently made his maiden speech in the House of Representatives. Still there was a strong distrust of theologians in Virginia, and it was feared that by the presence of a popular divine in the Convention the element of religion might be mixed up with topics sufficiently exciting in themselves. But the course of ALEXANDER CAMPBELL soon dispelled all such fears. He indeed belonged to a sect the most numerous in the Union—a sect, however, most devoted to religious freedom in its largest sense;—but, if it had been otherwise, of this powerful sect Campbell was a schismatic. There was no danger to religious freedom from him. He needed it more than any body else. With the doctrines of his church and with the constitution of the State he was equally at war. In his personal appearance, in his dress and manners, in his style of speaking, he was a man of the world; and it would not have been suspected that he was other than a layman, if in his speech on the basis he had not drawn his illustrations at length from the Jewish system, and sought to strike out George Mason's constitution with a view of inserting the book of Deuteronomy in its stead. He had a great fund of humor, and, observing the zeal with which the East pressed the antiquity of the constitution, he proved easily enough the superior age of his own system, and urged that the East on its own principle might without self-abasement lay George Mason at the feet of Moses. He was a fine scholar, and, with the younger members of the body who relished his amusing thrusts, his pleasant address and social feelings rendered him very acceptable. As a controvertist he had some great qualities; he was bold, subtle, indefatigable, and as insensible to attack as if he were sheathed in the hide of a rhinoceros. He made a successful rejoinder to Randolph, who had quoted in English the maxim of Lord Bacon : Time is a great

innovator; to which Campbell replied by quoting the entire maxim correctly in the original: Maximus innovator
tempus ; adding *quidni igitur tempus imitemur ?* He was a
native of Scotland, and, as he landed on our shores, he
happened to take up a paper containing a recent message
of Mr. Madison, which, he said, gave him the first impression of American genius. With the exception of Col.
Bierne, he was, I think, the only foreign-born citizen in the
body.

He was followed in the discussion by JOHN SCOTT,
whose speech on the basis was an able and well-timed
effort in favor of the East. It had not been his wont, to
use his own expression, to sing hosannahs to the constitution ; and his capital defence of the mixed basis came with
redoubled power from one, who, while, like Joynes and Upshur, he favored important changes, was willing sooner to
renounce them all than yield one tittle of his ground on that
question. Without the slightest pretension to any grace
of manner or style, with a voice harsh and forbidding, he
was an animated and most impressive speaker. He was
about the middle height. His face had none of that bright-
ness which irradiated the countenance of Morris, who preceded him on the side of the East in the discussion, but
seemed worn with disease, under the severe pressure of
which he made a renunciation of all public office forever ;—
a renunciation, which his subsequent election to a judge-
ship, the duties of which he discharged for ten or fifteen
years until the time of his death with acknowledged ability,
compelled him to revoke. He was a member of the federal party, and in the debate on the judicial tenure he
spoke with great force in opposition to Mr. Giles, between
whom and himself there was a sharp personal collision.

Although in the contests of the Convention the lines of
division were strictly drawn between the friends and op-

ponents of the old constitution,—now that those strifes are past, and most of the active spirits of that exciting time are no more, it may not be inappropriate to class two names together, which, though never on the same side on the perpetually recurring call of the roll, were bound by the chords of Christian affection, and were united in the support of all the religious and humane schemes which honored the age in which they lived—JAMES MERCER GARNETT and WILLIAM HARRISON FITZHUGH. Garnett was by many years the elder of the two, and may be said to have closed his political life twenty years before the assembling of the Convention, and before that of Fitzhugh had begun. He had been a member of the House of Delegates and was a member of the House of Representatives during the entire second term of Mr. Jefferson's administration ; and, though rarely engaged in prolonged debate, was an efficient coadjutor of the party at the head of which was Mr. Randolph, which opposed the policy of that statesman. Thenceforth he almost renounced public life, and devoted his time to agriculture, education and religion,—three great interests which then required all his fostering care. He was not far from sixty, but retained in his gait the elasticity and erectness of a young man. He did not make a formal speech during the session, but watched the progress of events with the strictest attention ; and some one present may remember how distinctly his sonorous voice was heard above all others at the call of the ayes and noes, and recognised at once. He was full of life, and delighted in society, of which his polished manners, his humor deepening at times into a caustic wit, and his large historical recollections, made him a brilliant ornament. If John Randolph excited the mirth of the Convention at the expense of Mr. Jefferson's "mouldboards of the least possible resistance," Garnett brought forth roars of laughter in private circles at Mr.

Madison's scheme of hitching the bison to a plough. It was in the social gatherings that the artillery of his political party was brought to bear with the most decided success; and many a young politician, who would have taken the alarm at an allusion to the embargo or the war, sunk under the raillery played against the philosopher and the farmer. His writings on agriculture and education have been long before the country, and, if they do not exhibit great attainments in any department of knowledge, reflect that homebred sense clothed in the simplest Anglo-Saxon garb, and that abiding love of his species, which were the conspicuous traits of his character.

The mind of Fitzhugh had probably received an earlier training, and was, perhaps, of a higher order. Even before he entered William and Mary he had studied the art of public speaking, and one of his surviving classmates yet speaks with rapture of his brilliant speech on the first occasion of his attending a society of that institution. He had long devoted himself to the cause of education and religion, and had gained honorable distinction a year or two before by his speech in the House of Delegates on a proposition to remodel the distribution of the interest of the Literary Fund on large and liberal principles. He was an early and steadfast friend of the Colonization society, and his controversy with a writer supposed to be Mr. Giles under the signature of Opimius in defence of that association attracted much attention at the time; and it is in his letters written on that occasion that some of the rich fruits of his genius may be found. His speech on the basis exhibited respectable powers, and was marked rather by that sound sense and truthfulness, guided by firmness of purpose, which constituted his character, and by his persuasive elocution, than by that subtle logic which was the order of the day. He was in the prime of life, of winning man-

ners, and was the pride and joy of every circle in which
he moved. He probably never made an enemy. In Virginia, where few of our eminent men have been conspicuous in the offices of religion, a prejudice, perhaps a rem-
nant of chivalry, still sticking to the skirts of the politician,
who may sit at the card table or over the bottle without
derogation from self respect or intellectual rank, leads him
to connect weakness of intellect with a tender humanity
and a high sense of religious duty. Fitzhugh, who, by the
way, had nothing of the Norman about him but his fine
proportions and the name, stood on the same platform on
the score of intellectual accomplishments and wealth with
the proudest of his fellows, and had a merit of his own.
He superadded the glory of a Christian Statesman. In
politics he embraced the doctrines of the federal school,
and dearly did he love to sit at the feet of its living Gama-
liel. Of the strictest temperance in all things, and in the
full enjoyment of those blessings which embellish life and
make it useful, a long and honored career seemed to ex-
pand before him; but, in the inscrutable will of Provi-
dence, he was destined to an early grave.

The name of yet another of the distinguished men who
had not been abroad in any public capacity, but whose long
and useful career at home, especially in the Senate of Virginia, was familiar to his countrymen, demands a grateful
commemoration. Such was the massive strength of his
intellect, so intimately were commingled in his character
all the finest elements of beauty, moral worth, and a lofty
patriotism;—so connected and endeared was he in the ten-
derest relations of life with so many persons on either side
of that mighty Ridge which has too long reared its icy bar-
rier between hearts which otherwise would have been, and
ought ever to be, united in the bonds of the strongest affection,—that I tremble as I approach the name of CHAP-

MAN JOHNSON. In a former sketch allusion was made to a brilliant galaxy of genius which adorned the college of William and Mary at a particular era. The name of Johnson suggests the recollection of a youthful triumvirate who were likewise associates in that venerable institution, who also chose the bar as a field of fame, and who, having attained almost all the highest honors which their country could bestow, cherished in age the cordiality of earlier years. I need hardly add that I speak of Philip Pendleton Barbour, Benjamin Watkins Leigh, and Chapman Johnson.* At the date of the Convention Barbour alone had been abroad, but all three had been bred in that school of the prophets, the House of Delegates under the old Constitution. Johnson was born in Louisa, and was, I believe, a son of the person of that name who has come down to us in an amusing caricature by the Marquis of Chastellux. When therefore he returned from Augusta to reside permanently in Richmond, it was a reclamation to which the East had an equitable title, and which it was proud to make. His position in the Convention was delicate and peculiar; for, like Stanard, he had received his appointment from the generous confidence of the friends of his early manhood. While he remained in the Senate as the representative of the Augusta district, so great was the general confidence in his integrity, he was regarded essentially an eastern man; and, although during the session of 1816 he had strenuously upheld the Convention bill, which was lost in the body of which he was a member by two votes only, yet he forthwith embraced the bill re-arranging the senatorial districts, and in a spirit of peace, and in opposi-

---

* I have learned since the delivery of this discourse that Robert Stanard was at William and Mary during a part of the college course with the persons whose names are mentioned in the text. Why does not William and Mary publish a triennial catalogue?

tion to some of his colleagues of the West, secured its passage. Believing the representation of the West in the
House of Delegates substantially fair, he was resolved, as
the Senate had been reconstructed, to oppose any future
efforts in favor of a Convention. Hence from that time
he ranged on that question with a great majority of the
people of Eastern Virginia, and gallantly sustained the
celebrated Substitute which his friend Leigh proposed at a
meeting of the citizens of Richmond instead of the report
and resolutions in favor of a convention which had been
offered and which were finally adopted. With these facts
fresh in the public mind, and with the belief that, though
elected by the people of Augusta, he was left free to pur-
sue the dictates of his judgment, it is not at all a matter of
surprize that the Eastern people generally expected him,
if not to sustain their peculiar views, at least to occupy
some middle ground on which both of the great parties
might fairly stand. But his course in the legislative committee soon dispelled these expectations; and when it was
known that he sustained the extreme measure of the West,
there was much disappointment, and the suspicions which
Mr. Randolph used with such effect, were, at a time of
high excitement, freely expressed. But the subject ad-
mits of an easy and satisfactory explanation. It has been
stated that he voted for the Convention bill of 1816, when
his main reason for so doing was the inequality of the representation. When, however, he had succeeded in secu-
ring the passage of the bill re-arranging the senatorial districts on the basis of white population, he obtained all that
he then desired. With the other parts of the constitution
he was not disposed to quarrel. But the re-arrangement
of 1816 was altogether a temporary measure; for, as the
country had outgrown the previous arrangements, so it
might be expected to outgrow that of the bill of 1816,

which, as it was based on the census of 1810, may be said to have borne on its shoulders the burden of six years as soon as it was born; but, believing that in 1829 that period had not yet arrived, he opposed a call for a Convention. Thus far consistency required him to go, but no farther. But when the question arose, not concerning a temporary re-arrangement of the Senate, but the establishment of a permanent basis of representation in the House of Delegates as well as in the Senate,—if consistency were called in, it would have sustained him in upholding the white basis in both houses, which was more than he contended for, as he was willing to concede a mixed basis for the Senate. Moreover, as no man is ready to sacrifice his honor without an equivalent, what had the West to bestow upon him? A seat in the General Assembly, a seat in the Council, the office of Governor or Judge, or even a seat in the Senate of the United States? Not one of these honors would he have accepted, had it been offered by the West, or the East, or both united. The reasons which brought him to Richmond would have kept him there. With all who knew the integrity of the man, such injurious suspicions weighed not a feather in the scale. Sir, if he were not guided in his conduct by a conviction of duty, then magnanimity and an exalted sense of honor are the mere bye-words of a vain philosophy. If we were permitted to look into the recesses of his great mind, it may be that the glorious vision of pouring oil upon that troubled sea, and of winning the reputation of a mediator among warring brethren, may have flitted before him. Of all the members of the body he was best qualified by position, experience, and weight of character, to perform such an office. He had frequently performed it in the Senate, and he might have hoped to perform it on a more solemn occasion. And, if the resolution offered by Tazewell, which regarded the existing constitution as a bill open to amendment, had been adopted, the scene might have presented itself. The adoption of that resolution would have been soothing to the feelings of the East. It would have shown that our brethren of the West believed that there was something in our institutions, which had borne the impress of two centuries, worth preserving. And, even if the basis of qualified voters, which Mr. Johnson was ready to propose, had been adopted, it is possible that a senate of fifty members on the federal basis, with a concurrent instead of a joint vote in all elections by the Assembly, would have satisfied a majority of Eastern men, who would have gained more real advantage by accepting such a scheme which, as it contained within itself the means of a future re-adjustment of the basis of representation, would have settled the public mind for half a century to come, than by adopting the arbitrary arrangement of 1830, which contained in its birth the seeds of its dissolution at no distant day. But no such policy prevailed. Every thing was to be torn from its foundations. And a state of feeling soon arose that bade defiance to all attempts at pacification.

His speech on the basis question, which consumed nearly three days in the delivery, which is reported with some degree of accuracy in the published debates, and which is one of the few speeches of his which are accessible by the general reader, was, as might well be expected, something more than an ordinary production. None but a person intimately conversant with the domestic policy of the State from the earliest period could have made it. While it presents an interesting view of our past legislation in illustration of his main topic, it preserves the prominent characteristics of his eloquence. Great courtesy, respect for the feelings of his opponents, and an unfeigned humility, which set off in bolder relief his great qualities, marked all his efforts. In the course of his general argument he was sometimes led to dwell too long on incidental topics, and apply to the weaker that time and strength which would have been more wisely expended on the leading parts of his subject. Hence, although it must be distinctly admitted that a minor topic sometimes assumed from incidental circumstances a dignity which it might not now seem to deserve, and required an enlarged illustration, yet his speech on this occasion, though at times he was very great, as well as his speeches at the bar, lacked that strength and compression which were the forte of his compatriot Stanard, as they lacked that brilliancy which flashed upon you in the speeches of Leigh. His mode of speaking was unique. He began in a tone almost inaudible, and gradually rose, sometimes in the course of a single sentence, to the highest pitch of his voice. To those who listened with delight to the flowing tones of Morris, the lively elocution of Upshur, the musical fulness of Leigh, and the rich soprano of Randolph, the management of his voice was often something less than pleasing; and to strangers who heard him for the first time, it was almost startling; but to those who were familiar with his manner, this peculiarity was almost overlooked, and his real excellence was apparent. He was more disposed to be grave than witty or sarcastic; yet he once made a happy retort on Mr. Randolph who replied to some remark of his with wanton severity; " Sir," turning to Mr. Randolph whose shrivelled face and shrunken form gave point to his retort, " Sir, it needs no ghost to tell me that." It is singular that his face, with the peculiar turn of his head when he was speaking, resembled that of the bust of Demosthenes so nearly as to arrest intent attention. When he addressed a friend, a benign smile, which lighted up his features, told the lovely character of the man. He rarely took an active

part in federal politics, and I am not aware that, with the
exception of the Adams Convention which was held in
this city in 1827, the address of which to the people of
Virginia was from his pen, and of the meeting which was
also held in this city in 1834 on the subject of the removal of the deposites from the Bank of the United States,
that he meddled with them at all in his latter years. He
never filled any office abroad, but retained to the last the
confidence of the General Assembly, which honored itself
by committing to his hands the preparation of the proposed new code. It was a fortunate opportunity for such a
man, whose fame was so purely Virginian, to follow the
example of his " noble friend from Chesterfield," and in-
terweave his own name indissolubly with the jurisprudence
of his country; but, after repeated efforts, he was compelled by indisposition to decline the office ; and, before
the new code appeared from the younger and more vigorous hands to which it was committed, his gentle spirit had
passed away. When the life and services of this excellent
man shall be weighed in the balance of history,—come
that day when it will—posterity will pronounce his reputation one of the purest and most precious gems in the
moral diadem of his native commonwealth.

With the name of Johnson was associated in the public
mind that of one not the least distinguished of the eloquent
triumvirate heretofore mentioned, who was not only his
classmate in college, his colleague in the General Assembly, his rival in the contests of the forum, and his compatriot in the political struggles of a long life, but the friend
of his bosom :—BENJAMIN WATKINS LEIGH. There was
such a community of fellowship, of genius, and of exalted
worth between these eminent men, that the name of the
one instantly brought to the lips the name of the other.
Until the Convention assembled, they had always acted in

unison with each other; but now they were not only to differ on the most exciting topic of the times, but to lead the columns of their respective forces. It was in the close quarters of the legislative committee, and not in the house, that the severest collisions occurred between them; but the flame of early friendship, to the honor of human nature be it said, though it seemed, as may presently appear, during a season of excitement unparalleled in our history, at times to flicker, burned with undiminished warmth to the end of their honored lives.

As with Johnson, so it was with Leigh,—he was returned from a district which he had served in early life, but in which he did not reside. His brilliant career in the Assembly and at the bar, his honorable mission to Kentucky, the skill and taste, and withal the scrupulous fidelity with which he had prepared the code of 1819, and his burning patriotism on several memorable occasions, had added no common lustre to his name. But it was in the Convention of 1829-30 that his genius shone with more than its meridian splendor. Virginia had long cherished him as one of her sons most distinguished for the strength of his reasoning powers, the fervor of his eloquence, and the unsullied purity of his patriotism, and it was hardly anticipated that he would do more in his new sphere than sustain his great reputation. She was mistaken, and not Virginia alone. His extraordinary displays not only dazzled the eyes of his fellow-citizens, but created wonder and admiration throughout the Union. A learned professor of a Northern University observed to the person now addressing the chair, that an able jurist, himself illustrious for his talents and for the grace with which he wore the highest honors of his native state, and who had mingled with the most eminent Virginians in Congress, declared to him that, great as were the men Virginia had sent to the federal councils,

she had retained at home, as if incapable of choosing
wisely, a statesman who far surpassed them all. However
equivocal in one respect this compliment may appear, it
was the opinion of a competent and an impartial judge,
and showed the impression which Leigh had made upon
superior minds abroad.

It will be remembered that the initiative was given to
the business of the Convention by the appointment of four
grand committees to which all the members of the body
were assigned; to one of these, the legislative, of which
Mr. Madison was chairman, Mr. Leigh was appointed. Of
this committee, the members of which were selected through
the courtesy of the President by their colleagues of the
Senatorial district as best qualified to maintain their interests on the greatest question likely to engage the deliberations of the body, it would be proper, if time allowed, to
speak at length. It held its sessions in the Senate Chamber of that day, to which all flocked, although there were
then sitting in the Capitol three other committees over
which presided Judge Marshall, Governor Giles, and Mr.
Taylor of Chesterfield. At the head of a long table, looking northward, sat Mr. Madison, while the other members,
in seats originally taken by chance, but retained throughout the session, were ranged about it, with the exception
of one member, who, as if to avoid even the appearance
of aiding in the dissection of a friend in whom life was not
extinct, and whom he still indulged the hope of rescuing
from the hands which were dabbling in its blood, sat apart
in the northwest corner of the chamber, his eyes almost
constantly fixed on a map of Virginia suspended near him,
and seeming seldom to stray from its eastern portion. I
need not say to the thousands who day after day watched
his slightest motion, that I allude to the orator of Roa-
noke, who, long the marvel of his countrymen, had never

before filled an office in the commonwealth, and was hitherto seen in the metropolis in passing only.   Rarely was
so great a number of eminent men to be seen in so small
a compass.   Besides the venerable Madison, who, as was
justly said, was not only at the head of that committee but
of the Convention, and was the .patriarch of the Union,
and Mr. Randolph, there was Tazewell, whose noble head
and flowing locks a Powers or a Galt would have selected
as his choicest model of Milton's human face divine, and
whose overshadowing reputation was then at its zenith;
Johnson, of whom I have just spoken; Mercer, a veteran in
public life, long known in the Assembly and in the House
of Representatives, in both of which bodies he held the
front rank ; reputed to be a foeman worthy of the steel of
Leigh with whom ere this he had grappled full often, and
directly in front of whom he now sat ; his mild expression
and graceful appearance typyfying, in some measure, his
chaste and fascinating eloquence ; Doddridge, the particular champion of the West, of whom I have already spoken,
watching with intense interest every movement of the
master-spirits of the East who were clustering about him ;
Tyler, already honored with the highest offices which the
state could bestow, and whose elevation to the Presidency
of the United States has made his person and mind familiar to all ; Mason of Southampton, then in the perfection
of manly beauty ; one of the rising statesmen of the day,
and, his career in the state councils yet unfinished, destined not only to [a seat in Congress and on the federal
bench, but to preside at a glorious epoch over one of the
most important departments of the federal government,
and whose recent appointment to the French Mission has
met with universal acceptance ; Green, the successor of
Roane on the bench of the Court of Appeals, whose name
will go down to posterity in connexion with one of the

most memorable debates on record, but whose modest appearance gave no indication of the high judicial merit generally accorded him ; Cooke, thin in stature, the full expression of a good face neutralized by green glasses; unknown in federal politics, and as yet in state, except as the author of a violent pamphlet in favor of the West which was distributed among the members of the Assembly at its last session ; his mind thoroughly imbued with the logic of the schools, and feeding on abstractions as its daily bread; versed in the minute history of the state, and famous for the provoking pertinacity with which he worried an opponent, a dog-eared Hening in his hand ; Joynes, large and grave, in goggles of portentous size, unknown in public life, but fitted for the highest civil employments, and as familiar with our finances as if they were the playthings of his childhood ; whose figures of arithmetic were the sworn foes of all figures of speech; Summers, a judge of the General Court, marked by great amenity of manners; who was supposed to hold divided empire with Doddridge over the affections of the extreme West; Roane, next to Madison, venerable in years ; whose public life dated back to the days of Washington ; Bierne, the muscles of whose honest face were anon convulsively twitched to sharpen a defective sense of hearing, which, however, did not prevent an active career in the Assembly and in Congress ; whose long and successful devotion to the pursuits of a merchant and a planter never obliterated a taste for the classic studies which beguiled his earlier years; Broadnax, whose tall and graceful person, draped in black, was conspicuous even in a sitting posture; more prominent at the bar than in public life ; Pleasants, who had been a member of the House of Delegates in '98-'99, and '99-1800, and subsequently its Clerk, a member of the House of Representatives and of the Senate, and Governor of the State, and in every sphere, by the blandness of his manners, his unsullied integrity, and his attractive eloquence, had won the esteem of his countrymen; Pendleton, who bore not only the name but the majestic form of that illustrious man, who presided in the convention of 1788, whose impress is seen over our whole history, and who in extreme age had closed his still active career almost within the shadow of the building in which his namesake was now sitting; and others whom I pass over in this hurried sketch, but who were entitled, if it were for their position on that committee only, to high consideration.

In such a body, the elite, I had almost said, of the Convention, the Virginian who was acquainted with the history of the state, and who loved eloquence, intuitively singled out Watkins Leigh; for his countenance, which must have been handsome in youth, still retained much of its freshness, and but that, with the exception of the glossy black hair that covered his temples, he was bald, he would have readily passed for a much younger man than he really was. He had a good forehead; and his dark eyes, when he was excited, seem to sparkle. His voice was sweet, and its volume ample enough for his style of address. His gestures were few and graceful, and mainly, as if in the act of demonstrating a proposition, with his right hand, which was small enough to have won the favor of Lord Byron or his friend Ali Pacha, and which, with his general form and especially his baldness, he inherited from the maternal side of his house. Like Byron, he was lame, from an accident however but, such was the elegance of his manners, the defect, if it did not heighten, did not impair the dignity of his demeanor. It is remarkable that his colleagues Giles and Jones were also lame;—a fact that gave birth to a jest among the younger members in strong contrast in one sense with the true state of the case, that the

Chesterfield district had sent the lamest delegation to the body.

The ball in committee was barely in motion, when Mr. Leigh took the lead among the eastern members, and gallantly did he keep it until the final adjournment. Some of the finest specimens of his eloquence might have been selected from his unpremeditated outbursts around that council board; but I regret to add, that, unless in the slight memoranda made at the time by the person addressing the chair, they are lost forever. He ran over the gamut of parliamentary debate; and argument, wit, sarcasm, pathos, were perpetually at his service. He never missed his mark; and once when he assailed with irresistible humor a position of Johnson's, that gentleman sharply observed that he had appealed to the wisdom, not the wit of the committee. There was one occasion in committee, when the various qualities of Mr. Leigh's eloquence were exhibited with great brilliancy and effect. Judge Green had offered a proposition in favor of the mixed basis, and Leigh had sustained it with an animated speech, which was replied to by Mercer and Johnson. To these Judge Green replied but in a tone so low as not to be distinctly heard. Mr. Cooke also opposed the proposition in a very able speech in which he detailed for the first time his elaborate abstractions on the subject of government. The array was very formidable to any speaker, but never did Mr. Leigh acquit himself with greater eclat. He began by saying that the gentleman from Loudoun (Mercer) had misapprehended or misrepresented him. He did not say that representation was apportioned to taxation under the articles of confederation. He said that when the question arose in framing those articles the North contended that the capitation tax should bear equally upon black and white, bond and free, which the South objected to; and that the question was settled at last in 1781 on the three-fifths' principle. He then stated that this was an argument urged for engrafting the principle in the present federal constitution, and by the writers of the Federalist for its adoption by the people. To prove his statement he referred to the 54th number of the Federalist (written by Mr. Madison, as that gentleman afterwards avowed.) He then proceeded to argue that no government was safe that did not protect property; that the definition of property was that the substance of the possessor was *his* to retain or dispose of as *he* thought proper, and demonstrated that this could not be the case in a government in which the majority had not an amount of property equal to that possessed by the minority. To show his distrust of such a government he drew an illustration from the case of his brother. I have, he said, a brother whom I dearly love, and in whose integrity I repose unlimited faith. But do you imagine that I would deliver even into his hands while I had life in my body, and while my wife and children look up to me for support, all my estate, or, what is tantamount, assent to give him the power of leaving me penniless in the world? No, sir, I would not do it. None but a simpleton would do it. I mean no personal allusion; but I say none but a simpleton would assent to such a government; none but simpletons ever assented to such; and the law that acted on this principle acted only on simpletons, natural idiots, mutes, and the whole generation of *non-compos* people. (Here a loud and convulsive laugh burst from the committee and from the crowd in the lobby. Mr. Madison elongated his upper lip, and assumed a serious air that was irresistibly comic. Randolph, who in the isolated position I have described appeared wholly inattentive to what was passing, but was in fact the closest observer in the room, seemed for the first time since the body met evidently amused, while the

opponents of Mr. Leigh showed that they felt the force of
his logic and the play of his wit.) He continued: The
gentleman from Frederic (Cooke) exhorted us to disregard
sectional interests and act like statesmen; that is, we must
disregard *local* interests. Sir, I assure that gentleman that
I, for one, will not disregard the interests of my constituents in Chesterfield. I will never consent—never—while
they pay one hundred cents and his constituents fifty seven
only, to deliver them over to his tender mercies. I choose
rather (looking closely at Cooke) to follow the example of
the gentleman than his precept. (A laugh) As to the refined abstractions of that gentleman, he would not banter
them with him now. The gentleman from Loudoun (Mercer) has proposed guarantees for our protection. I have
no confidence in guarantees—none whatever; and least of
all do I believe they would be observed by gentlemen who
construed the plainest, simplest words in the world opposite to their plain and palpable meaning. (An allusion to
Mr. Mercer's federal politics. Another laugh from the
committee and from the lobby.) The gentleman from Augusta (Johnson) flatters us with the belief, that, if we are
soft enough to adopt the white basis, the East would still
preponderate in the legislature from the superior education
of her sons. I deny it altogether; I deny that any man
has been half-educated in Virginia since the Revolution,
(a laugh), and, as to his guarantees, I have no confidence
in them where property is concerned, any more than I have
(to use a phrase not "of strict rhetorical propriety") in
that high obligation higher than the constitution itself
which has recently been the theme of public explanation.
(An allusion to Mr. Johnson's defence in the address of the
Anti-Jackson Convention of a famous expression of Mr.
Adams.)

Far be it from me to intimate that I have made a tolerable sketch of the speech itself; but I am disposed to think that it may to a certain extent support the opinion that there was a finer field for the display of brilliant powers of debate in the close quarters of the legislative committee than in the Convention itself, where from the excessive length of a speech which occupied several days, the scene became rather a contest of dissertations, especially on the basis question, than a field of legitimate debate. What forcibly struck the observer of Mr. Leigh's course in committee was his readiness in discussion. He was never taken by surprise; and when some unexpected movement, as was frequently the case, changed the aspect of affairs, he displayed, what great experience and ability often fail to do, that self-possession, that two-o'clock-in-the-morning courage, which Napoleon ascribed to Massena. The writers on the theory of government he had studied in early life, and retained his knowledge; and when Mercer spoke of Locke's reply, instead of Sidney's, to Sir Robert Filmer, a glance of Leigh's eye told that the speaker had missed his mark. But it is time the committee should rise. As I recall those scenes, I seem to see their living forms fresh before me. The tones of their eloquent voices yet linger on my ear, and I can almost feel the stifled breath of the crowd that thronged the lobby and encroached on the floor; and in another moment I appear to move among the graves of the departed. When I remember the social converse of those eminent men, which it was my privilege to enjoy, and reflect that it seems but yesterday I saw them about that council-board or heard the voice of wisdom from their lips, I shrink from the havoc which death has made in their ranks. Out of that single committee Madison, Randolph, Doddridge, Broadnax, Bierne, Pleasants, Roane, Summers, Green, Chapman, Taliaferro, and Campbell of Bedford, have finished their course on earth, and the grave has but lately closed over the gallant forms of Johnson and Leigh.

It was, however, on the floor of the Convention itself. that Mr. Leigh made those displays which attracted so much of the public attention toward him. The debates in the legislative committee, pungent as they were, were but the skirmishes that preceded the general engagement, and that engagement was the longest and most animated that was then known in our history. It has been stated, that, as soon as the resolution of the committee basing representation in the House of Delegates on white population exclusively was called up, Judge Green moved to amend it in favor of the mixed basis;—Upshur, as before observed, opened the debate in splendid style, and was followed by speakers from East and West successively, who displayed a thorough knowledge of the subject and great powers of eloquence. But it was left for Mr. Leigh to pronounce a speech which was a map of the whole subject, which discussed principles, and refuted objections to the existing constitution unanswerably at least in the opinions of its friends, and which impressed the large audience that eagerly crowded to the hall during the two days of its delivery with a degree of admiration rarely excited by forensic efforts. Nor was this his only great speech; for he was the warder on the watch-tower of the East; and no topic, great or small, urged against the constitution or the East, but was met by him and almost invariably with triumphant success. His knowledge of the past history of the state, even of a local or temporary kind, was wonderful and he was equally at home in discussing the alledged misconduct of the Council in allowing a few pounds of damaged gunpowder to be used for a salute on some public occasion, and what he supposed to be the true nature of Bacon's rebellion. His style of speaking was impressive.

His voice, as before observed, was music itself, and his eloquence seemed at times to gush from his lips almost without articulation, and to come directly from the heart ; for, what added much to his weight of character, he was serious in his purposes, and he believed himself struggling in defence of all that in his opinion rendered Virginia dear in the estimation of others and in his own. He said to a friend that in early life he studied Burke, but that in his latter years he adopted Swift as his model ; and the union of the styles of these two writers may give some notion of his own ; for, though his severe logic never would have allowed him to indulge in the diffusive eloquence of Burke, his imagination ever burned brightly, and he was especially fond of Anglo-Saxon words, as he was, indeed, of the Anglo-Saxons themselves. The substitute offered at the Richmond meeting heretofore alluded to, is a fair specimen of his writing on a political subject, and is a noble commentary upon the old constitution, while his Christopher Quandary affords a graceful exhibition of his mode of writing on lighter subjects. While Mercer tripped in his allusion to Sidney, and was unfortunate in his quotation from Ovid, Leigh, though he quoted frequently, and sometimes at length, never went astray. The debates published by Mr. Ritchie will afford posterity a fair impression of his mode of argument and his topics ; but much was in his manner and in the occasion, which, however impressive at the time, can never be recalled. I have spoken of his prominent position as the great leader of the East; but it ought to be said, that his authority extended to the minutest details of forms. I remember when the President, the late Judge Barbour, himself thoroughly versed in the logic of parliaments and in all their forms, was about to sign the enrolled bill of the new constitution, which was placed on the Clerk's table before him, some doubts arising in his mind about the proper mode of signing it, which those standing near him were anxious to remove, he observed: No, gentlemen; let us wait till Leigh comes; he knows more about these things than any of us.

To trace the course of Mr. Leigh through a session of three months and a half would require a volume; but, such were his extraordinary powers, that he retained his influence undiminished to the last. This is, indeed, no common praise. It is true that the distinguished talents of the East never shone with greater lustre than in the various discussions that arose in constructing the fundamental law; yet the toil and the responsibility mainly devolved on him. No project, no scheme, and they came in legions from East and West, but what was critically analysed by him, and he was as remarkable for his diligence in examining the details of the most complicated propositions as he was for the closeness of his reasoning and the elegance of his declamation. To attain and preserve such an ascendancy in such a body was a glorious achievement. Long were the eyes of the commonwealth fixed steadily upon him, and he well knew that not a word fell from his lips unwatched or unheeded. Had his life closed with the adjournment of the Convention, his apotheosis would have been without a parallel in our history. The East would have clothed herself in mourning, and been bathed in tears. Eloquence and poesy would have blended their chaplets on his insensate brow. The statue, radiant as the living original, would have leapt from the rock to memorialise the gratitude of his country, and to present to distant times the outward type of its benefactor. But he lived—lived to render yet farther and most valuable service to the whole people, and alas! to see a change come over them, and, I fear, to feel it keenly.

It was from the peculiar caste of his character that any

faltering of the public regard toward him would be sensibly felt. As a patriot of enlarged views, perhaps, rather than as a politician, he had always enjoyed the confidence of the General Assembly, and it was a singular coincidence in his life that the only missions dispatched by Virginia since the adoption of the federal constitution to her sister states—the one to Kentucky, the other, at a long subsequent date, to South Carolina,—were unanimously conferred upon him, and that it was his good fortune to discharge them both with unqualified applause. He loved Virginia with a passion as pure and fervent as was ever cherished in a human bosom, and regarded her as the impersonation of all that was good and beautiful. With many men patriotism is a profession, at most a principle ; but with him it was a passion ; and such was its intensity, that I verily believe he loved the vices as well as the virtues of his idol, and would have fought as readily in defence of her prejudices as of her principles. There was no alloy in his love of country. I may add, what gave additional elevation to the platform on which he stood in the Convention was, not only the purity of his private life, his distinguished services, and his professional reputation, but the general belief that he would not descend from his position to assume office however exalted, or to curry favor for future honors. None saw more clearly than he did the future predominance of the " backwoods vote," as the Western vote was ominously termed by Mr. Johnson, and he knew the effect proximate and remote of every word that he uttered ; but his mettle was such that the danger of any duty was a propelling motive to its execution. He was quick in temper, and his chivalry prompted him to meet an opponent with the weapon of his choice, but he was not inexorable. When he had stricken his foe, his noble nature would have recoiled from the use of the tomahawk and the

scalping knife. Like all truly great men, he was easy of
approach, and, although it was impossible not to feel in
such a presence, it was plain he sought no adventitious
means of heightening respect or inspiring awe, for he was,
as much as any man living, above all the tricks which
little men use to bolster a reputation ready to perish with
the passing year. He well knew that his reputation, if it
were worth having, would take care of itself. His heart
was sensible to all the gentle emotions; he dearly loved
his friends, and he avowed in debate with a candor that
softened the rancor of the sentiment, that he was too apt
to hate his enemies.

He may be said to have leaned to a past age more than
became so great a mind. Not that he did not bring his
fine faculties to bear wisely and promptly on current topics;
but his heart seemed to be with by-gone times. Like those
speakers in the British Parliament, who, overlooking the
present, perpetually recur to a period when their constitution so called existed in all its purity—a period the wit of
man has never yet ascertained—Mr. Leigh dwelt on the
glory of Virginia before the Revolution, and seemed to
cherish the prejudices of the old cavalier as warmly as if
he had lived in past times and had just landed on our
shores a fugitive from Marston Moor or the fatal field of
Worcester with a Cromwellian flea in his ear. It would
have been a choice intellectual treat, could one have heard
him under the full excitement of debate overhaul Carlyle's
book on Cromwell, and discourse on the modern mode of
making new saints out of old sinners. He was no fervid
believer in human progress, and one would infer from the
remark heretofore quoted about education, and which reflected his prejudices, that the country had rather retro-
graded than otherwise in knowledge since the Revolution,
while the opposite opinion is unquestionably true. The

colonists must have been educated, if at all, abroad or at home. If abroad, where were those wholly educated men in the Revolution? Who was Washington, Henry, Mason, Wythe, Pendleton, Jefferson, Madison? men who were the cloud by day and the pillar of fire by night through that perilous struggle? Men who had never left their native land. And Richard Henry Lee was more indebted to his own application in the colony for the development of his powers than to a short residence at a provincial school in Yorkshire. And if the Colonists were educated at home, what other public institution did they possess than William and Mary? and wherein was that superior to the same William and Mary under Madison, Empie, or Dew, Washington College under Graham, Baxter, Marshall, or Ruffner, Hampden Sidney under the Smiths, Alexander, Hoge, Cushing, or Maxwell, Randolph Macon under Olin, Doggett or Smith, or the University from its establishment to the present day? Where are the evidences of this high intellectual culture? Where are the books, tracts, speeches, poems, of the ante-revolutionary epoch? It is remarkable that Mr. Jefferson, who sought to furnish a list of the literary works of the colony, when he had enumerated Beverly and Stith, overlooking, by the way, that pearl of our early literature, the translation of Ovid by Sandys, could only produce a pamphlet by Col. Bland; and it is probable that the colony of Liberia has published more newspapers since its establishment than were published in Virginia from the settlement at Jamestown to the passage of the resolutions against the stamp act. While it is improper to assent to the unmingled praises of the past, it would also be unwise to overlook the idiosyncrasy of those who indulge the mood. Such opinions are in some degree conservative of what is valuable as well as what is worthless, and exercise an influence on affairs not to be despised;

yet it is questionable whether they flourish most in minds of the highest order.   Wo unto philosophy, and progress, and the welfare of the human race, if it were otherwise ; and honored, forever honored be the names of Bacon, Locke, and Jefferson.

When allusion was made to the mortification Mr. Leigh might have felt by the action of the General Assembly, to pass over federal politics, I referred to the loss of his election as a judge of the Court of Appeals.   The East might have conferred that appointment as a crowning honor on the man who had proved himself her boldest defender in her darkest hour, and was confessedly the first lawyer in her realm, but she virtually gave it to another.   The time may not be distant when the great battle may be renewed once more ; and, when the clouds of the coming tempest are closing round her, she will remember to whom she owed so much on a similar occasion, and will bitterly regret her ingratitude ; and then she will shed the grateful but unavailing tear on the grave of Leigh.   And if, hereafter, the Court of Appeals, like the French Academy, shall gather the busts of the distinguished jurists who have sat upon its bench to adorn its hall, and should the image of Leigh appear within those precincts where his living presence ought to have been felt, the proudest judge that ever sat on that bench may well inscribe on the lifeless marble what Saurin wrote on the bust of Moliere : Nothing was wanting to his glory, *he* was wanting to ours.

It is time that I draw to a close.   And, although I have not spoken, unless incidentally, of the living, I must pass over the names of Bayly and Henderson, Coalter and Mc-Coy, Jones and Wilson, Nicholas and Naylor, Pleasants and Summers, Trezvant, Venable, and others who participated in the debates, and whose lips are now sealed in death.   Nor have these alone fallen.   Twenty-four years form no inconsiderable proportion of the whole term of human life. In that interval I have more than doubled my own years. Those members, then in the first flower of manhood, whose brows have since borne or bear your greenest laurels, are now treading the brink of old age. Of the ninety six members whose names were reported to the house from the committee of elections thirty seven only survive. Dade and Read did not live to take their seats in the body, nor did Watson ever appear. Mennis was the first of the qualified members who met the King of Terrors. He grew ill, resigned his seat, and went home to die. Macrae died immediately after the adjournment, and before the close of the year Giles was no more. Monroe survived the adjournment a year and a half, and died at the residence of his son-in-law in the city of New York on the most memorable day in our annals. Marshall, who had endured an excruciating disease at intervals for some years, died five years after in the city of Philadelphia, whither he had gone for medical assistance, but was fortunately spared the agony of learning the death of his son Thomas, also a member of the Convention, who was struck by a falling chimney as he was passing through the city of Baltimore to visit his dying father, and instantly killed. Randolph survived three years, and in the city of Philadelphia, where his political career had begun thirty four years before, far from those patrimonial trees which now cast their shadows over his grave, breathed his last. Madison outlived his two distinguished compeers. and died six years after the adjournment in his classic home. There was no watcher by the bed side of the lamented Barbour. He had retired in his usual but always delicate health the night before his death to his room in a boarding-house in Washington, and when he did not appear at the breakfast table in the morning, his associate judges, who were then

holding their court in that city, and who lodged in the same
house, hastened to his chamber to behold the mortal remains only of their beloved colleague. Doddridge died
also in Washington. Upshur perished by the terrible ex-
plosion of the Princeton, when Virginia wept the fate of
more than one of her distinguished sons. Trezvant died
on the banks of the distant Mississippi. The ashes of the
gallant Taylor of Norfolk repose not far from the spot
where the remains of his brave soldiers, who fell by the
hand of disease, were deposited, and beneath the turf over
which he had marshalled the batallions of his countrymen
at the most trying period of the last war with Great Britain. Venable, the fragrance of whose memory will ever
be fresh on the banks of his beloved Appomattox, died instantly as he was walking through his fields. Leigh and
Johnson died within a year of each other in this city.
Stanard fell, as it were, on the field of his fame. He had
heard the argument of an important case in the Court of
Appeals, and retired to his study to prepare his opinion,
which, drawn with all his eminent skill, he had nearly concluded, when, as he drew toward its close, the letters seemed to be indistinctly formed, the words were slightly con-
fused, and presently the pen is seen to stray from its course
in the unfinished line, as the angel of death suddenly summoned him to that higher court before which the glories of
earth are as the shadows that pass away.* And within
the past year, Samuel Taylor died from a fall at the Dan-
ville depot in this city, and Taliaferro has also departed at
an advanced age. Of these, Madison, Marshall, Monroe,
Venable, and Taliaferro, alone attained the three score
years and ten of the Psalmist.

---

* The case was Yerby and wife vs. Lynch, 3rd Gtrattan, 517, where the
opinion of Judge Stanard as far as completed may be found.

In regarding the mortality of the members, it would seem at first sight to exceed that of the federal convention of 1788 in a remarkable degree. The federal convention, as gathered from the vote on the ratification of the constitution, consisted of one hundred and sixty eight members, and in 1829, when our Convention assembled, a space of forty one years, there were five survivors: Mr. Madison, Mr. Marshall, Mr. Monroe, Judge Stuart of Augusta, and James Johnson of Isle of Wight. This would give an annual average of about four deaths in forty one years. The Convention of 1829 consisted of ninety six members originally elected to the body, and approached nearer one-half than two-thirds of the members of the former body. Yet in twenty-four years, out of that number fifty nine have died, or considerably over one-half, at a rate exceeding two each year since the adjournment; and when the relative numbers of both bodies are regarded, the mortality of the convention of 1829-30 would seem nearly double that of the Convention of 1788. On the other hand, if the life of the Convention of 1788 is to be measured by the life of the latest survivor, a different result will follow. James Johnson, the last survivor, died at his residence in Isle of Wight in 1845 at the age of ninety nine years; and thus a period of fifty seven years passed before the entire extinction of the members of that body;—which would make an annual average of two deaths only. If the last test, which seems to be the true one, be adopted, it will be many years, I trust, before the relative mortality of the two bodies can be determined. The Convention of 1776, that framed the constitution which our convention was called to revise, consisted of about one hundred and fifty members, and became extinct in the death of Mr. Madison in 1836 ; a period of sixty years, which would give an annual aver-

age of two and a half per cent. of deaths in that interval.*
It must be admitted, however, that the data necessary to
form a correct conclusion on such subjects are so compre-
hensive and difficult to ascertain, that all inferences drawn
from them are apt to be more curious than just.

It was on the fifteenth day of January, 1830, that the
convention, which then held its sessions in the Baptist
church below the Monumental, met for the last time. The
enrolled bill of the constitution was signed by the president, when, after the transaction of some business strictly
official, Mr. Randolph rose to offer a resolution in honor of
the president (who had called Mr. Stanard to the chair)
and spoke with a pathos in delightful unison with the occasion ; and when the president resumed the chair, and, before pronouncing the final adjournment, addressed the body
with a glow and grace that seemed beyond the reach of
his peculiar powers, many a tear was seen to fall from eyes
unused to the melting mood. The tide of party ran strong
and full during a session of more than three months, and
every one in and out of the convention felt more or less
the intensity of the excitement. But the time was come,
when old and young, friends and enemies, were about to
part to meet no more. No eye could have discovered the
cloud of death that hung black above them ; for none
thought of the young and vigorous so soon to fall ; but
every eye was fixed on a few old men of exalted worth
who would soon leave us forever ; and when the body ad-

---

* In the journal of the Convention of 1776 the list of members given is
altogether incomplete ; and, although the complement of the body may be
ascertained elsewhere, it cannot be known from the journal, as the ayes
and noes were not called during the session. In the convention of 1788,
the ayes and noes were called three times only ; while in the convention of
1829-30, they were called so frequently after the committees had reported,
that it is impossible to open the journal without seeing them, and they probably make up half of its bulk.

journed, all pressed to shake by the hand for the last time these venerable men of the past age. When the president concluded his address, he declared the final adjournment, and the convention of 1829-30 became among the things that were. And, although the structure of their hands has been re-modeled by those for whom it was reared, and most of those master-builders in the science of constitutional architecture, as they were termed by the president, have passed away, I trust that the office of pronouncing their names on the ear of the busy world—an office which a sincerely wish had been consigned to more competent hands—may not be without its use in stimulating the youth of Virginia to cherish the memory of their wisdom and worth, and emulate the glory which they have bequeathed them.

APPENDIX.

A list of the Members of the Virginia Convention of 1829-30, *reported October* 9, *by the Committee of Privileges and Elections.*

From the district composed of the counties of Amelia, Chesterfield, Cumberland, Nottoway, Powhatan, and the Town of Petersburg.

John W. Jones,*   Samuel Taylor,*
Benjamin W. Leigh,*   William B. Giles,*

From the district composed of the counties of Brunswick, Dinwiddie, Lunenburg, and Mecklenburg.

William H. Broadnax,*   Mark Alexander,
George C. Dromgoole,*   William O. Goode.

From the district composed of the counties of Charles City, Elizabeth City, James City, Henrico, New Kent, Warwick, York, and the cities of Richmond and Williamsburg.

John Marshall,*   Philip N. Nicholas,*
John Tyler,   John B. Clopton,

From the district composed of the counties of Shenandoah and Rockingham.

William Anderson,   Peachy Harrison,*
Samuel Coffman,   Jacob D. Williamson.

From the district composed of the counties of Augusta, Rockbridge, and Pendleton.

Briscoe G. Baldwin,*   William McCoy,*
Chapman Johnson,*   Samuel McD. Moore.

From the district composed of the counties of Monroe, Greenbrier, Bath, Botetourt, Alleghany, Pocahontas and Nicholas.

Andrew Beirne,*   Fleming B. Miller,
William Smith,   John Baxter.

From the district composed of the counties of Sussex, Surry, Southampton, Isle of Wight, Prince George and Greensville.

John Y. Mason,   Augustine Claiborne,*
James Trezvant,*   John Urquhart.*

From the district composed of the counties of Charlotte, Halifax, and Prince Edward.

John Randolph,*   Richard Logan,
William Leigh,   Richard N. Venable*.

From the district composed of the counties of Spotsylvania, Louisa, Orange and Madison.

James Madison,*   David Watson,*
Philip P. Barbour,*   Robert Stanard.*

From the district composed of the counties of Loudoun and Fairfax.

James Monroe,*   William H. Fitzhugh,*
Charles F. Mercer,   Richard H. Henderson.*

From the district composed of the counties of Frederic and Jefferson.

John R. Cooke,   Hierome L. Opie,*
Alfred H. Powell,*   Thomas Griggs, Jr.

From the district composed of the counties of Hampshire, Hardy, Berkeley, and Morgan.

William Naylor,*   Elisha Boyd,*
William Donaldson,*   Philip C. Pendleton.

From the district composed of the counties of Washington, Lee, Scott, Russell, and Tazewell.

John B. George,   Edward Campbell,*
Andrew McMillan,*   William Byars.

From the district composed of the counties of King William, King and Queen, Essex, Caroline, and Hanover.

John Roane,*   Richard Morris,*
William P. Taylor,   James M. Garnett.*

* Dead.

From the district composed of the Counties of Wythe, Montgomery, Grayson, and Giles.

Gordon Cloyd,*
Henley Chapman,*
John P. Mathews,*
William Oglesby.*

From the district composed of the counties of Kanawha, Mason, Cabell, Randolph, Harrison, Lewis, Wood, and Logan.

Edwin S. Duncan,
John Laidley,
Lewis Summers,*
Adam See.*

From the district composed of the counties of Ohio, Tyler, Brooke, Monongalia and Preston.

Charles S. Morgan,
Philip Doddridge,*
Alexander Campbell,
Eugenius M. Wilson.*

From the district composed of the counties of Fauquier and Culpeper.

John S, Barbour,
John Scott,*
John Macrae,*
John W. Green.*

From the district composed of the counties of Norfolk, Princess Anne, Nansemond, and the borough of Norfolk.

Littleton W. Tazewell,
Joseph Prentis,*
Robert B. Taylor,*
George Loyall.

From the district composed of the counties of Campbell, Buckingham, and Bedford.

William Campbell,*
Samuel Claytor,*
Callohill Mennis,*
James Saunders.

From the district composed of the counties of Franklin, Patrick, Henry, and Pittsylvania.

George Townes,
Benj. W. S. Cabell,
Joseph Martin,*
Archibald Stuart.

From the district composed of the counties of Albemarle, Amherst, Nelson, Fluvanna, and Goochland.

James Pleasants,*
William F, Gordon,
Lucas P. Thompson,
Thomas Massie, Jr.

* Dead.

From the district composed of the counties of King George, Westmoreland, Lancaster, Northumberland. Richmond, Stafford and Prince William.

W. A. G. Dade,*   John Taliaferro,*
Ellyson Currie,*   Fleming Bates.*

From the district composed of the counties of Mathews, Middlesex, Accomac, Northampton, and Gloucester.

Thomas R. Joynes,   Calvin H. Read,*
Thomas M. Bayly,*   Abel P. Upshur.*

A List of the Members who Voted on the Final Adoption of the Constitution.

The names of the gentlemen who voted in the affirmative, are: Messrs. P. P. Barbour,* *Pres't.* Messrs. James M. Garnett,*

John W. Jones,*   John S. Barbour,
B. W. Leigh,*   John Scott,*
Samuel Taylor,*   John W. Green,*
William B. Giles,*   Thomas Marshall,*
William H. Broadnax,*   Littleton W. Tazewell,
George C. Dromgoole,*   George Loyall,
Mark Alexander,   Joseph Prentis,*
William O. Goode,   Hugh B. Grigsby,
John Marshall,*   William Campbell,*
John Tyler,   Samuel Branch,*
Philip N. Nicholas,*   George Townes,
John B. Clopton,   Benj. W. S. Cabell,
John Y. Mason,   Joseph Martin.*
James Trezvant,*   Archibald Stuart, Jr.,
Augustine Claiborne,*   James Pleasants,*
John Urquhart,*   William F. Gordon,
John Randolph,*   Lucas P. Thompson,
William Leigh,   Thomas Massie, Jr.,
Richard Logan,   Fleming Bates,*
Richard N. Venable,*   Augustine Neale,
James Madison,*   Alex. F. Rose,*
Waller Holladay,*   John Coalter,*

* Dead.

Richard H. Henderson,* Thomas R. Joynes,
John R. Cooke, Thomas M. Bayly,*
John Roane,* Abel P. Upshur,*
William P. Taylor, William K. Perrin,—55.
Richard Morris,*

And the names of the gentlemen who voted in the negative, are:

Messrs. William Anderson, Messrs. S. M'D. Moore,
Samuel Coffman, Andrew Beirne,*
Peachy Harrison.* William Smith,
Jacob D. Williamson, Fleming B. Miller,
Briscoe G. Baldwin,* John Baxter,
Chapman Johnson,* Robert Stanard,*
William McCoy,* Charles F. Mercer,
William H. Fitzhugh,* Gordon Cloyd,*
Joshua Osborne, Henley Chapman,*
Alfred H. Powell,* John P. Mathews.*
Thomas Griggs, Jr., William Oglesby,*
James M. Mason, Edwin S. Duncan,
William Naylor,* John Laidley,
William Donaldson,* Lewis Summers,*
Elisha Boyd,* Adam See,*
Philip C. Pendleton, Charles S. Morgan,
John B. George, Alexander Campbell,
Andrew McMillan,* Eugenius M. Wilson,*
Edward Campbell,* Samuel Claytor,*
William Byars, James Saunders.—40.

Mr. Doddridge was absent at the call of the ayes and noes.

* Dead.